MOTION PICTURE PIONEER:

The Selig Polyscope Company

By the Same Author

Continued Next Week
World of Laughter
Kops and Custards
Bound and Gagged
Clown Princes and Court Jesters (with Sam Gill)
Collecting Classic Films
Winners of the West
Dreams for Sale
Ladies in Distress
Mack Sennett's Keystone
Collecting Vintage Cameras
Glass, Brass & Chrome
Gentlemen to the Rescue
Riders of the Range

MOTION PICTURE PIONEER:

The Selig Polyscope Company

Edited by
KALTON C. LAHUE

South Brunswick and New York: A. S. Barnes and Company
London: Thomas Yoseloff Ltd

A. S. Barnes and Co., Inc.
Cranbury, New Jersey 08512

Thomas Yoseloff Ltd
108 New Bond Street
London W1Y OQX, England

Library of Congress Cataloging in Publication Data

Lahue, Kalton C   comp.
  Motion picture pioneer.

  1. Selig Polyscope Company. I. Title.
PN1999.S4L3   338.7′61′79143   75–37824
ISBN 0-498-01103-8

Printed in the United States of America

Contents

Preface

The early motion picture companies have been sadly neglected in writings of the cinema, yet they contributed heavily to the growth and maturity of the movies in America. The use of contemporary source material to help tell the story of the Selig Polyscope Company (not that of its founder, William N. Selig) adds immeasurably to the flavor of the story and provides an insight into both the making of the early Selig films and the enthusiasm of those for whom they were made. Trade papers of the era were carefully searched for representative materials and the contents then cross-checked with known facts to prevent legends from slipping in as fact. This method of documenting an era seems preferable in telling the story of the Selig Polyscope Company and has the added value of providing ready source material to which the average reader has only limited access, if any at all.

With rare exceptions, the Selig Polyscope films have over the years almost completely disappeared; therefore many of the firsts that the company can lay claim to are unavailable today. Thus the sampling of illustrations from its productions represents an important asset to all those interested in the early cinema, as very few of the films themselves are likely to be resurrected in the coming years. The purpose of this volume, then, is simply to document that portion of an era which in only a little more than half a century has disappeared virtually without a trace.

The Selig Collection at the Academy of Motion Picture Arts and Sciences was consulted extensively and many thanks must be extended to DeWitt Bodeen of the Academy's staff, as well as to Winifred Greenwood, Eugenie Besserer and Bessie Eyton, all now deceased.

MOTION PICTURE PIONEER:

The Selig Polyscope Company

1
The Selig Polyscope Company

The founder of the Selig Polyscope Company was a large, dignified (despite his background) and somewhat reserved gentleman who enjoyed the unreserved affection of nearly all his employees over the decade and a half of his company's active existence. Born into a lower middle class Chicago family on March 14, 1864, William Nicholas Selig was educated in the Chicago public schools but surprisingly little else is known of his early years. By the time he was 19, Selig had moved to California, supposedly because of ill health, where he took up a career as manager of a health spa while effecting a cure. About 1894, this young man, who often indulged his fancy for parlor magic, took to the road, billing himself as "Selig, Conjurer." From this his act developed and expanded into a minstrel show attraction that also provided him with the appelation of "Colonel."

Seeing Edison's Kinetoscope for the first time in a Dallas peep show parlor in 1895, Selig's inventive mind was captivated by the possibilities inherent in the magic lantern that projected moving pictures upon a wall. Folding up his act, Selig returned to Chicago, where he took modest lodgings at 43 Peck Court and began experimenting. To finance his new project and conserve his funds, the showman-turned-entrepreneur opened a commercial photographic shop specializing in carbon prints and enlargements for clients, many of whom were railroads. Working with samples of Edison's films during this time, Selig was getting nowhere in devising a practical projection apparatus when both the Latham and Lumière[1] projectors turned up at Chicago's Schiller Theatre. Acquiring samples of the films used in these devices, Selig continued his quest with renewed vigor, frequenting the Union Metal Works for machine shop assistance.

It was there that he discovered drawings of the Lumière Cinematographie, a dual camera-projector. An unknown customer had brought in various parts for Andrew Schustek to duplicate, and as time passed the various working drawings began to take a definite shape and form. Despite the customer's insistence upon absolute secrecy, Schustek realized that he was constructing a new Lumière machine, one piece at a time. When Selig caught a glimpse of the drawings, he conferred with the machinist and the two men decided that there was little harm in pursuing the project further. Schustek took additional shop facilities at the corner of Chicago's Western Avenue and Irving Park Boulevard, where the project was begun, and in time the Selig Standard Camera and its companion projector, the Polyscope, were devised. Schustek became the sole producer of the equipment, with Selig as his one customer. While Edison owned major patents on the fledgling motion picture camera and projector, and contested in court those he didn't, Selig felt confident that he could and would escape both the at-

---

1. Major Woodville Latham and Louis Lumière had both achieved projection with systems somewhat different than that of Edison. Latham's famed "Loop" became a stormy center of controversy in many early litigations.

11

William N. Selig in 1941; age 77. Trade paper editors complained constantly that of all the prominent men in the industry, only Selig and Frank Marion of Kalem preferred to remain unphotographed.

tention and legal wrath of the Wizard of Menlo Park—after all, wasn't his Polyscope based upon the French Lumière design?

The Selig Multoscope Company became the Selig Polyscope Company, and in 1896 Selig made his first motion pictures. For the most part, these were short films (25 to 50 feet) of a topical nature and sold to vaudeville houses in Chicago. The business gradually prospered in the next decade as Selig, taking no chances upon the generosity of Thomas Edison, took to the road for extended trips into Colorado and the Southwest where he filmed scenics, many of which were made for the popular Hale's Tours. Story films were not neglected after Edwin S. Porter's *The Great Train Robbery* in 1903; G. M. Anderson, soon to find fame as co-founder of Essanay and the movies' first cowboy star, was hired as a producer in 1904 and took a tour into the Southwest where he filmed several western stories for Selig, but ever-cautious and feeling the watchful eye of Edison's legal counsel over his

shoulder constantly, the Colonel was not yet willing to commit himself to the open defiance of challenging Edison on home territory. He had started with virtually nothing and built a modest business by being careful. Sales of his camera and projector, while not spectacular, had provided a basis for the operation, but in the years after 1903 Edison became more and more determined in his efforts to remove those who intruded upon his domain, regardless of the source of their inspiration. Unlike American Mutoscope, which had openly challenged Edison, Selig was content to remain in his own little corner of the empire, cautiously bidding his time and consolidating his resources.

In the period 1905–07, Edison moved fast and hard against his competitors and Selig's activities became the object of injunctions and lawsuits with which he was ill-equipped to cope. In the best melodramatic tradition, help from an unexpected quarter arrived at the last moment. Some years before, Selig had taken movies of various meat packing processes at Philip D. Armour's Chicago plant, using liberal quantities of whitewash to help in the reflection of light. It so happened that Armour was also in trouble at this time; Upton Sinclair's muckraking novel *The Jungle* had aroused storms of controversy about the packing industry, and searching for a reply to what he naturally felt were vicious and unfair allegations, Armour recalled a man named Selig and his peculiar-looking black box. A trip to 43 Peck Court confirmed his hunch; the Selig pictures would provide a more than suitable answer to his critics.

But Selig was in no position to be of help; Edison had won an injunction that forbade Selig from doing

A facsimile of Selig's business card used in the years before he joined the minstrel circuit.

exactly what Armour needed—making further prints. Undaunted, Armour struck a bargain with Selig; in return for sufficient prints, his legal staff would undertake the defense of the producer's case. This move was preordained to failure, but it did save Selig from going under and bought him time, which proved to be a most precious commodity, for there were other forces at work.

H. N. Marvin of Biograph and George Kleine, a Chicago importer of European films, were attempting to reason with Edison and their efforts ultimately culminated in the formation of the Film Service Association, a combination of producers and exchanges licensed by and through Edison that sought to bring an end to the internecine warfare that had characterized the growing motion picture business while enriching Edison's bank account without the commensurate drain of legal fees. At best it was a truce, but by January 1909 it would evolve into the Motion Picture Patents Company, with Selig firmly ensconced as a member in good standing.

In 1907, Selig had enlarged the activities at Western Avenue to include a primitive studio and hired a well-known stage director, Francis Boggs, to produce films. Boggs joined Selig in the fall of that year and immediately set forth on the road, following the well-traveled route into Colorado with a group of actors, photographing films as they went along using the natural scenery for backdrops. But Boggs went on to California, where he finished shooting a single reel version of *The Count of Monte Cristo* (1908) near Laguna and Venice. Returning to Chicago, Boggs was outfitted for another trip and left for New Orleans in April 1908 with Tom Santschi, Jean Ward, James L. McGee and Harry Todd. James Crosby went along as cameraman, and once again Boggs extended his trip to take the company back to California. This sort of traveling production was engaged in by all those seeking to escape the wrath of Edison, but Boggs was the first to establish permanent quarters in California. By the end of 1909, Selig had four producers operating three full-time facilities—Boggs in California, Louis J. Howard in New Orleans, and Otis Turner and Frank Beal in Chicago. The Chicago studio had grown considerably and Selig had moved his offices out of the tenderloin to 45–49 East Randolph Street.

The Film Service Association had established set prices for films—13 cents per foot, with standing order prints at 11 cents minus 10%—and required ex-changes to return to it each six months an amount of film equal to that purchased in the previous semiannual period. With its licensing procedures formalized in the Motion Picture Patents Company, it provided a neat package, from producer to exchange to theatre, and guarded against any unauthorized use of the footage produced and sold. Only those licensed to use the equipment and films provided by the Association and later the Patents Company could deal in rental and/or exhibition of movies without fear of prosecution, and while the trust set in motion a great maelstrom of discontent among those not included in its arrangement —and one that would eventually contribute heavily to its own downfall—for William N. Selig and the others involved it was a godsend.

Francis Boggs had recommended that Selig establish permanent California facilities, an assessment in which the producer concurred, and in March 1909 he arrived in Los Angeles where space was rented in the rear of a Chinese laundry on Olive Street, between 7th and 8th Streets. Thus the first film to be made completely in California was a Selig effort released July 27, 1909, as *The Heart of a Race Tout*. From these temporary quarters, Boggs moved to Edendale, then a quiet suburb of Los Angeles, and began the construction of a permanent studio in August of that year. James L. McGee became its general manager and Boggs its creative genius.

By 1910, business was so good for the Selig Polyscope Company that its founder ordered the enlargement of both the Chicago and Edendale studios. At the former, he spent $75,000 to erect a new 80- by 120-foot three-story building; the first two floors housed an addition to the processing facilities, a carpenter shop, dressing rooms and a property room, with the third story serving as a new studio. At Edendale, $20,000 was spent to construct a 60- by 120-foot building, and in mid 1911 this was expanded to 230 by 220 to incorporate new offices and the growth of supporting facilities like properties, wardrobe, etc.

Selig now embarked upon the course of events that would provide handsomely for his care and needs long after he left active production. For some years after the 1908 court decision had established the precedent of screen rights,[2] he had been purchasing stories from

---

2. Kalem had filmed the Lew Wallace novel *Ben Hur* in one reel and the Wallace estate brought suit, winning a $25,000 judgment that virtually ended piracy of story material by early movie makers.

both noted and unknown authors, usually for $50 or so, although competition soon forced rates up to $100 per reel and more. As cheap as this sounds today, it was a financial windfall for many of the authors. Early in 1911, The Selig Polyscope Company contracted with Street and Smith, well-known pulp magazine publishers, for exclusive scenario rights to all stories which they published, and the burgeoning scenario files in Chicago were placed under the direction of Kenneth Langly as editor. Noted authors like Elbert Hubbard, Opie Reed and William V. Mong sold their story rights and then joined Selig's scenario staff, which included Chris Lane, J. Edward Hungerford, Charles E. Nixon and Arthur Tobin.

Under publicity manager T. H. Quill, the Selig Polyscope Company pioneered the five-color advertising one-sheet, selling them directly to theatres for a dime apiece. Advertising heralds were made available to theatres at a nominal cost for distribution to their patrons, and a variety of well designed, neatly printed advance notices of forthcoming releases were sent out weekly to a large mailing list of exchanges and theatres.

By the close of 1910, the Selig Polyscope Company had built a small but select stock company of actors that included Paul W. "Tom" Santschi, Betty Harte (whose real name was Daisy Light), Hobart Bosworth, Charles Clary, Kathlyn Williams, and Herbert Rawlinson. The most distinguished and best-loved of the Selig actors, Bosworth was acquired by Boggs for the lead in *In the Power of the Sultan,* a 1909 release. Born in Marietta, Ohio, on August 11, 1867, Bosworth had run away to sea at age 12 and three years later traded his sailor's life for that of an actor in a San Francisco stock company. He became a Broadway idol before he was 30, but the first decade of the new century had been a hard one; ill with tuberculosis and low in fianances, he had been forced to leave the stage and move West in search of a more healthy climate. Having sufficiently recovered to return to work, Bosworth became a stage director for the Belasco Theatre in Los Angeles, a position he left to open a dramatic school in partnership with Oliver Morosco (and one occupied by Herbert Rawlinson just prior to his joining Selig). The school was not a success and Bosworth was once more in financial need when approached by Boggs and McGee. The outdoor work involved in

making movies proved healthful and the actor-director settled upon this new career, writing 112 of the scenarios and directing 84 of the 140 films in which he appeared for Selig before leaving to found his own company in 1913 to produce Jack London's *The Sea Wolf.* For a man resigned to dying in 1900, Hobart Bosworth proved a remarkable specimen, working in the industry until 1942, just a year before his death at the age of 76.

Kathlyn Williams was a Butte, Montana, girl who came to the movies from the stage via Biograph in 1910, joining Selig that same year. She remained with the Polyscope Company until 1916, when Selig's fortunes had ebbed to a point where he could no longer afford her services. The best-known and most popular actress on Selig's player roster, Miss Williams became primarily identified with the wild animal stories made in Chicago and on location in Florida. The California studio leads were handled mainly by Bessie Eyton, a gorgeous Santa Barbara girl whose versatility before the camera was proven weekly as she appeared with Tom Santschi and Bosworth in virtually every role from Indian maiden to ingenue to fishwife.

Tom Mix joined in 1910 while acting as advisor for a quasi-documentary, *Ranch Life in the Great Southwest,* and while he functioned for several years under producer-actor William Duncan, he came into his own as writer, director and star by 1914. Nominal head of various Selig ventures in Colorado in 1912, Duncan established a studio at Canon City with Marshall Stedman where he filmed western adventures and comedies. Wheeler Oakman and Harold Lockwood joined the roster in 1911–12, giving the producing staffs in Chicago and California strength and popularity. One of the most popular actresses was little Lillian Wade, who came to the screen in *One of Nature's Noblemen* at age two. By the time she was four, Baby Lillian carried many films virtually by herself, often working with young Roy Clark, son of character actor Frank Clark.

The Selig Polyscope Company suffered its first major setback on October 27, 1911, when William Selig, who was in Edendale to confer with the contractors about a studio addition, was wounded in an attack by a Japanese gardener on the studio staff; Francis Boggs was killed. The tragedy began when Otto Breitkreitz, the animal tamer in charge of Selig's growing menagerie, discovered Frank Minnimatsu peering through the keyhole of Boggs's office about 10:00 A.M. Breitkreitz's sudden appearance frightened the gardener, who fled into Hobart Bosworth's empty dressing room before he could be questioned. This room also led into Boggs's office and a few minutes after the hour, several shots echoed through the corridors, bringing Tom Santschi and E. H. Philbrook (secretary and treasurer of the Edendale studio) hurrying to the director's office. Breaking down the door, Santschi found Minnimatsu about to make his exit into the studio proper, Selig clutching his arm and Boggs's still form resting in a heap at his feet. Pursued by Santschi and Philbrook, the gardener ran into the studio and fired again, this time at Bessie Eyton who was seated awaiting a call to go on-set. Fortunately for Miss Eyton, he missed. The rugged Santschi then closed in and overpowered him with ease; the pistol was now empty.

Boggs died enroute to the hospital; Selig's shoulder wound was superficial and more painful than dangerous. But the Selig Polyscope Company had lost its best-known and most prolific director to the gun of a fanatic who could furnish no reasonable motive for the slaying, and his passing was genuinely and deeply felt by all in the growing Hollywood film colony. Exactly how great a loss his death really was to the company is difficult to assess; the cinema was far too young and his output, although great, has not survived the passing years. Boggs was working in an era when stage reputations were important to a director and there is little doubt that he was well-known and respected, but his career ended before he had a chance to do anything of real importance. Colin Campbell, who took his place, eventually proved to be the most important of Selig's directors.

The following articles carry our story of the Selig Polyscope Company through 1916, providing an insight into the production of early motion pictures. Of especial interest is the recounting of how Selig, a staunch Republican, miffed when ex-President Theodore Roosevelt sailed for Africa without taking a Selig cameraman with him, faked a filmic account of the safari in his Chicago studio and released it to an unsuspecting public as *Big Game Hunting in Africa*, complete with advertising materials that prominently featured an unknown actor made up to look like Theodore Roosevelt. Such oddities were favorite Selig subjects at the time; as a Mason, he filmed regional and national convocations of the Shriners, releasing them and other unusual subjects as independent specials. Our selections range through the years 1909–1916 and are accompanied by appropriate photographs; those appearing with the original articles have been deleted because of their poor reproduction qualities.

Selig used these small advertising heralds during 1905–08. For a 335-foot film (running time under four minutes), the synopsis is remarkably detailed. In the space stamped The Selig Polyscope Company, exhibitors could have the name of their theatres printed at a slight additional cost.

Supplement No. 90 and 91, March, 1908.

"FRIDAY THE 13th"

(A gloom-dispelling innovation of disasterous comicality.)

Length, 660 Ft.   Price $79.20

Code Word: FRITH

"SWASH-BUCKLER"

(Miltons Bully Vagabond Gentleman.)

Length, 335 Ft.   Price $40.20

Order by Title

THE SELIG POLYSCOPE CO.

FRIDAY THE 13th.

Profusely abounding in facetious aptitude and appeasing constituency, so superlatively humorous that some portion, or the other, is sure to delight any one whomsoever, this production is truly the cream of comics; a rare sort of giggle producer, chucked full of fun.

The hero—more appropriately, the victim—encounters as hazardous a lot of mishaps as could befall any martyred individual with a degree of safety for life or possible avoidance of fatal injury.

The first section of soothing scenography affords the only interval for a long breath. A maid is busy about the dining-room of a well furnished home, is late with breakfast, everything goes wrong and she superstitiously points to the calendar which shows the date to be *Friday the 13th*. She worries over this discovery and becomes *more* confused. The mistress enters and shows decided anger because the morning meal is not served. Then hubby enters, (This is where the "big noise" begins because he is *the funny man*); he—the victim—is already late at his office, and insists on breakfast being brought forth immediately. Everything served is only half cooked and consequently tough. He frets at this, then burns his fingers on a hot dish—in fact, on several hot dishes, is also superstitious about the weird looking calendar date, becomes more annoyed and excited, tucks the table-cloth under his chin in his confused search for a napkin, gets up hurriedly, pulls the tab e-cover with him, upsetting all the dishes. This makes him so sore he kicks the table over, then seeks composure from a cigar which proves to be an ill weed. The maid appears, he tries to take his spite out on her, but is thoroughly antagonized in this attempt. His wife is far from sympathetic over his misbehavior and when he leaves the house she follows him. He falls in the snow just outside the door, sees his wife and "lights a rag," with his heart's idol in close pursuit.

Next the victim tries to catch a car to get down town, misses it and is next seen in conflicting unison with the snowy street. He then sees two men in a fighting argument. They exchange their rights a couple of times and he intervenes by shoving them apart. Both are angered at this interference and throw him in a snow-heap, head first, sufficiently hard to break his corpus callosum, but still actively intent upon getting to his office, he hires a bicycle, which turns out a failure, is bruised considerably, and throws the wheel from him with such fierce disgust that the tires come off. Succeeding this he hires an express wagon, drives it himself, frantically, runs amuck, gets out and upon seeing the wagon's number to be 13, almost prostrates. Goes further and appropriates a delivery sled, makes another reckless drive, turns a sharp corner and is thrown head over heels in a snow bank. (Mgr. Note—This was a dangerously hard fall, and an unintended one, but shows up swell.)

He finally gets to the office, so lame that he sends for a pair of crutches. But he is still able to get "mushy" with his young lady office assistant; at which point the wife arrives. Catching him engaged thus blissfully, she immediately proceeds to flag him with an article of umbrellic diameter. The girl is frightened to a shrivel. Boy brings crutches and the victim starts for home, enthusiastically encouraged by his heart's idol, who energetically flogs him the best part of the way, if not all. He is next seen beaten to a frazzle, and laid out, with his crutch appurtenances, on the front steps of their suburban domicile.

Upon their return a message awaits them announcing the intended visit of his mother-in-law. The wife is vigorously vindicative toward this verisimilitude, but the victimized individual experiences a velocity of vicissitude in his mental vicinity which vibrates with no vehement viscosity of venial verse or shows any vestige of approval toward this veracious visitation of his vernacular relation—only stronger.

The fair maternal ancestor soon arrives, heading a procession of bundles, baggagemen and a trunk of ancient pedigree, which brings up the rear. (She is exceptionally clever in this role.) After several narrowly successful escapes, the victim succumbs to her cordial embraces, with extreme fear and anxiety, in which lovably consolidated state of affairs we leave them.

SWASH-BUCKLER.

Swash-buckler, the braggadocio of renown, was so called because of his perpetual tendency to bluster his valor and because of his redeeming feature to defend good from evil, for, as the picture shows, a good cause gave him a strong arm, and to some extent he maintained his boastful attitude. But his manner was a source of constant danger from which only friendship and timely good fortune saved him.

The finery and antiquity of the costumes and stage settings add remarkably to this production.

The first is a tavern scene where several men are at a table. *Swash-buckler* enters; his friends join him in drink.

Next scene shows where a villainous Captain of the Guard is beating a boy for some slight offense.

The boy, knowing *Swash-buckler* to be resentfully inclined, comes in and tells him. Captain and soldiers follow. *Swash-buckler* and Captain argue excitedly and a duel ensues in which *Swash-buckler* proves a master with the sword and kills his opponent. His friends disperse the soldiers, who later return and take *Swash-buckler* by surprise. With many guns leveled at him his sword is of no further avail.

The subsequent scene shows *Swash-buckler* in prison, where the boy comes to tell him he will take the bullets out of the soldiers' guns and save him from death, at the intended execution. The boy leaves and a Monk, accompanied by guards, enters the prison cell and reads the condemnation.

The following picture shows the boy out in the prison court removing the bullets and replacing the guns where he found them. The soldiers come after their rifles and then lead *Swash-buckler* out to be shot. They aim and fire at him with the blank loads, he falls as though killed. Monks carry him away on a barrier for dead. After they have arrived at their destination, *Swash-buckler*, to their intense surprise, arises and waves them out of his sight. Being greatly frightened they willingly and hurriedly comply. The finale shows *Swash-buckler* and the boy making good their escape.

Will release Thursday, March 19th.

Late in 1908, the heralds were increased in size and the films in length, but the synopsis remained quite complete.

Supplement No. 140   February 4, 1909

GET THE HABIT

A HIT *Selig's* **FILMS**

A WORD TO THE WISE
Prosperity
Follows all Selig Film Users.   Order Selig's Films

Stirring Days in Old Virginia

Released Feb. 4, 1909

The greatest war picture turned out.   Don't miss it

Code Word, Old Virginia.   Length 1000 feet

Order from Your Nearest Film Exchange

This film should live forever and always draw packed houses

THE SELIG POLYSCOPE CO., Inc.
45-47-49 E. Randolph Street   -   Chicago, Illinois

PACKED HOUSES ALWAYS

WATCH US GROW

Stirring Days in Old Virginia

A picture story replete with the grim realities of war. Our scenes occur at or near the Warren homestead a few miles from Petersburg, Va., time, March and April, 1865. The gigantic struggle for the maintenance of the Union has gone on for four years, untold treasure has been expended, human lives by the thousand have been sacrificed, and America, destined to be the mightiest nation the sun has ever shown upon is still in the throes of Civil War, that stern test fate seems to make necessary for all infant governments.

Grant and Lee, the two greatest generals of the opposing sides, are locked in what must prove for one of them the grapple of death. In war as in all else there must come a day when the end draws near and defeat or victory perches upon the opponent banners—it is in these stirring days that our story opens.

The first scene occurs in the yard of the Warren homestead, a stately Colonial mansion that has been a landmark for many hundred years in this section of Virginia. Capt. Warren, the present head of the Warren family, is with Lee, an officer trusted with secret missions. The Federals under General Logan of Illinois are encamped on the Warren plantation, and General Logan himself has taken up his quarters with his staff in the roomy old mansion. Mrs. Warren, the young and beautiful wife of the Captain, with a few faithful slaves, is allowed to remain.

General Logan is in close touch with his superior, General Grant, who is now in front of Petersburg, a new plan of attack is being formulated, the signal corps ride away with their orders, Captain Warren has managed to communicate with his wife after the Federals occupy his home and has asked for a disquire, a complete Federal officer's uniform; a faithful slave, old Zach, has secured it for him, and we see him conceal the clothes amongst the shrubbery about an old stone wall that passes the house. Then we witness the Signal Corps in drill field operation. Our scene then shifts to Lee's camp in the woods near Petersburg, a scout rides up to headquarters with startling news ——?

> "The enemy contemplate a new movement,
> We must be able to read their signals,
> A bold man might secure a code book at their
> Warren homestead Station."

Captain Warren is standing by. "Let me go, General, I know every foot of the ground." "It is a spy's work, Captain, and means death if you are captured." "I know the risk I run but my chances of success are good,

and think, General, what it means to you sir, to know their plans."
"You are the man we need Captain, you shall go." The staff salute the
Captain as he dashes away on his dangerous mission. To gain the out-
skirts of his own grounds, he dodges from bush to bush along the river
bank, he then gains access to an old woodshed some distance from the
house, a pre-arranged signal brings his wife and faithful slave Zach to
him, the disguise is given. After donning the clothes he boldly enters
the signal station, salutes the third operator, saying, "I've just arrived
from General Grant's headquarters. I'm to wait here for dispatches. If
you don't mind I'll snatch a few winks of sleep." "Help yourself," is the
reply and the spy sinks down upon a pair of steps behind the operator's
table and feigns sleep, the officer of the day calls and receives the last
tidings of the evening for General Logan. Salutes and leaves, the spy's
opportunity has arrived, the book he is risking his life to obtain, has just
been tossed within reach of his hand by the young officer who, after
looking up the meaning of a sentence, has returned the code to its resting
place on the table. To smash the unsuspecting operator on the base of
the skull with the butt end of his revolver, grap the book, dash out
through the window, mount his waiting horse and escape is the work
of a few frenzied moments for Captain Warren. A fusilade of shots follow him, the entire signal corps and their reserves are called out and
give pursuit. This moment has been foreseen and provided for by Captain Warren, a battalion of Confederate Infantry are in hiding barely a
mile from the signal station, keeping within sight of the pursuing soldiers,
Warren leads them into the trap, the entire corps are surrounded, and
in this dire extremity, the officer in charge, Major Geo. Devere, calls for
a volunteer to ride for reinforcements. A dashing young soldier of his
command, Lieutent Harold McFarland, takes the message, and securing
a loose horse whose owner, a Confederate soldier, has been tumbled from
his saddle by a well directed shot, he dashes for help. We see him ride
up to the sleeping camp of General Powell's Brigade, then the bugle
sounds and the sleepy soldiers spring to arms, and in 30 seconds after
McFarlands arrival, the troops are under way. Then comes the rescue
and thrilling battle scene. The Confederates attempt to retreat, but
overpowered by superior numbers, they in turn are surrounded and compelled to surrender, Captain Warren yielding up his sword to Young
McFarland, who brings his prisoners before General Logan, a search
reveals the stolen code book, the wounded operator is sent for and in
another scene we see Warren identified by the operator, and his sentence
as a captured spy follows: "Execute at day break," the order reads. The
Captain's wife is present when he is brought in a prisoner, and at day-
break next morning she encounters the stacked arms of the firing squad
against a wall in the rear of her home, with unfaltering courage. She

smilingly asks the guard on duty if he can't spare the time to take a warm cup of coffee, and with the help of her faithful allies, the table is brought out on the porch and placed in such a way that the unsuspecting guard is seated with his back to the guns. Old Zach, with his dear master's life depending upon his efforts, carefully extracts the bullets from the paper shells of the stacked rifles, while the wife keeps the guard engaged in conversation. A few minutes later the officers detailed to execute the spy leads out his prisoner, the guards enter, take up their guns, the Captain is mercifully blindfolded and placed against the wall, it is a trying moment for him, his safety depends upon his feigning death after the order is given to fire—this he does. The officer in charge takes his men to the supply tent for a stretcher and tools to dig a grave for the man they think they have executed. As they disappear around the corner of the house, Warren makes his way to where the half-fainting wife awaits him with a stolen Federal uniform, to don the clothes and pass the guard is the work of a few moments. The firing squad return for the supposed body of the spy, only to learn that they have been tricked and that Warren has made good his escape.

CLOSING DAYS.

The next eight scenes of this thrilling picture are utilized to show the closing days of the great Civil strife, both Warren and McFarland meet soldiers' deaths in the last pitched battle of the war. Then follows the field surrender of General Robert E. Lee to General U. S. Grant. After the surrender our story closes with the great emancipator's words to the victorious army, delivered at Richmond:

"The war is ended, let reconstruction begin." This scene has been faithfully posed from photographs of the period, and introduces Generals Grant, Logan and Sheridan, of the army of '65, also several members of Lincoln's famous war cabinet, and the great emancipator, Abraham Lincoln, America's Martyred President.

Order Posters
For This Great War Picture
10 cents

A facsimile of a Selig Polyscope contract issued to motion picture exchanges wishing to handle his films. Note the prices charged exchanges and the minimum rental schedule by which they agreed to adhere.

Form 565. 2-15-08.

MOTION PICTURE FILMS.

Prices, Discounts, Terms, Rental Schedule, Conditions of Sale and Agreement for United States of America.

SUBJECT TO CHANGE.

ISSUED BY

SELIG POLYSCOPE COMPANY

CHICAGO, ILL., U. S. A.

MOTION PICTURE FILMS.

Prices, Discounts, Terms, Rental Schedule, Conditions of Sale and Agreement for the United States of America.

SUBJECT TO CHANGE

ISSUED BY

SELIG POLYSCOPE COMPANY,

CHICAGO, ILL.

Prices of Licensed Positive Motion Pictures

List .... 12 cents per running foot.
Standing Order 1 print............ 11½ " " " "
    "   "   2 prints........... 11   " " " "
    "   "   3 prints........... 10½ " " " "
    "   "   5 prints........... 10   " " " "
    "   "   7 prints and over.. 9½ " " " "

A purchaser may give a separate standing order for each of his offices.

All prints for each seperate standing order will be shipped only to one office.

The price charged will be, for each office, according to the number of prints shipped to that office as per above.

Discount

The vendor will allow, on all the licensed positive motion pictures sold by vendor to the purchaser, prior to September 1st, 1908, a discount of 6% off the above prices for cash remitted on delivery of goods.

Terms

All shipments are made f. o. b. vendor's office at purchasers' risk. C. O. D. at the vendor's option.

Minimum Rental Schedule For Licensed Positive Motion Pictures

Price for Service   Weekly Contracts

WHEN CHANGED	1 Reel	2 Reels	3 Reels	4 Reels	5 Reels	6 Reels	7 Reels
Once a week.........	$16	$32	$ 48	$ 64	$ 80	$ 96	$112
2 times a week.......	20	40	60	80	100	120	140
3 times a week.......	24	48	72	96	120	144	168
4 times a week.......	28	56	84	112	140	168	196
5 times a week.......	32	64	96	128	160	192	224
6 times a week.......	36	72	108	144	180	216	252
EVERY DAY	40	80	120	160	200	240	280

Each reel must contain not more than eleven hundred (1100) feet.

In all contracts for less than 7 days, the price is $6.00 per day per reel.

EXHIBITOR TO PAY EXPRESS CHARGES BOTH WAYS.

Conditions of Sale.

Licensed motion pictures manufactured under re-issued Letters Patent No. 12,192, dated January 12, 1904, are sold by Selig Polyscope Company, hereinafter referred to as the Vendor, subject to the following conditions:

1. **From the date of this agreement,** the purchaser shall buy exclusively licensed motion pictures obtained from the vendor, or from a duly licensed manufacturer of such motion pictures, under said reissued Letters Patent.

2. **The purchaser shall not sell nor exhibit** licensed motion pictures obtained from the vendor, but shall rent out such motion pictures only to exhibitors, who shall exclusively exhibit licensed motion pictures obtained from the vendor or from a duly licensed manufacturer under said reissued Letters Patent, but in no case shall the exhibitor be permitted to sell or sub-rent or loan or otherwise dispose of said licensed motion pictures.

3. **The price to be paid by the purchaser to the vendor** shall in no case be less than that defined in the foregoing schedule of prices, or in any other substitute schedule of prices which may be regularly adopted by the vendor, and of which notice shall be given to the purchaser hereafter.

4. **To permit the purchaser** to take advantage of any standing order price mentioned in said schedule, said standing order shall remain in force for not less than thirty (30) consecutive days. An increase in the number of prints to be furnished on a standing order shall be considered as a new standing order and must be in force for not less than thirty (30) consecutive days. Any standing order may be canceled or reduced by the purchaser on thirty (30) days' notice. Extra prints shall be furnished to the purchaser at the price which the purchaser is paying under his standing order, in force at the time the extra prints may be ordered.

5. **The purchaser shall not sell, rent, or otherwise dispose of,** either directly or indirectly, any of the vendor's licensed motion pictures (however the same shall have been obtained) to any persons, firms, or corporations, or agents thereof, who may be engaged either directly or indirectly in selling or renting motion picture films.

6. **The vendor shall not make or cause to be made** or permit others to make, reproductions or so-called "dupes" of any of the vendor's motion picture films, nor sell, rent, loan or otherwise dispose of or deal in such reproductions or "dupes."

7. **The purchaser shall not deliberately, remove** the vendor's trademark or tradename or title from any licensed motion picture film obtained from the vendor, nor permit others to do so, but in case any title is made by purchaser, the vendor's name is to be placed thereon, provided, that in making any title by the purchaser, the vendor's trade-mark shall not be reproduced.

8. **The purchaser shall return to the vendor** (without receiving any payment therefor, except that the vendor shall pay transportation charges incident to the return of the same) on the first day of every month, commencing seven months from the first day of the month on which this agreement is executed, an equivalent amount of positive motion picture film in running feet (not purchased over twelve months before) and of the vendor's make, equal to the amount that was so purchased during the seventh month preceding the date of each such return, *with the exception, however,* that where any such motion pictures are destroyed or lost in transportation or otherwise, and proof satisfactory to the vendor is furnished as to such destruction or loss, the vendor shall deduct the amount so destroyed or lost from the amount to be returned.

9. **The purchaser shall not rent out licensed motion pictures** below the minimum rental schedule above set forth, or any substitute or substitutes therefor, which may be regularly adopted by the vendor, and of which the purchaser shall have notice.

10. **The purchaser shall not offer any inducements or concessions** in the form of premiums or rebates or furnish to the exhibitor any supplies or merchandise by which, either directly or indirectly, the licensed motion pictures will in effect be rented at prices below said minimum rental schedule.

11. **The purchaser shall not sell, rent, loan or otherwise dispose of** any of the vendor's licensed motion pictures (however the same may have been obtained) to any person, firm or corporation in the exhibition business, who may have violated any of the terms or conditions imposed by the vendor through any of its other vendees and of which violation the present purchaser may have had notice.

12. **The purchaser shall not rent out licensed motion pictures** to any exhibitor unless a contract with said exhibitor (satisfactory in form to the vendor) is first exacted, under which the exhibitor agrees to conform to all the conditions and stipulations of the present agreement applicable to the exhibitor; and in the case of an exhibitor who may operate more than a single place of exhibition, a similar contract shall be exacted in connection with each place so operated.

13. **This agreement is personal** to and non-transferable by the purchaser.

14. **The vendor agrees** that before making sales of any licensed motion pictures to any purchaser in the United States (not including its insular territorial possessions and Alaska) it will exact from each such purchaser, an agreement similar in terms to the present agreement, in order that all purchasers who may do business with the vendor will be placed in a position of exact equality.

15. **It is understood and specifically covenanted** by the purchaser that if the purchaser shall fail to faithfully keep and perform the foregoing terms and conditions of sale, or any of them, or shall fail to pay for any goods supplied by the vendor within the time prescribed for such payment, the vendor shall thereupon have the right to refuse to supply the purchaser with any further goods and shall also have the right to place the purchaser's name on an appropriate suspended list, which the vendor may publish and distribute to its customers, associates and the several licensed manufacturers under said reissued Letters Patent, and the vendor shall also have the right in such case to immediately terminate the present agreement, without prejudice to the vendor's right to sue for and recover any damages which may have been suffered by such breach or non-compliance with the terms and conditions hereof by the purchaser.

16. **It is understood that the terms and conditions of this agreement** may be changed at the option of the vendor upon sixty (60) days' written notice to the purchaser, but no such change shall be effective and binding unless duly ratified by an officer of the vendor.

AGREEMENT.

In Consideration of the sale of licensed motion pictures to me-us at net prices, to be agreed upon with the vendor, and which shall not be less than the prices mentioned in the foregoing Schedule of Prices, and after carefully reading the above Terms and Conditions of Sale, which together with said Schedule of Prices and said Minimum Rental Schedule are to be taken and read with and as a part of this Agreement, I-we Hereby Covenant and Agree with the vendor to conform with, and strictly adhere to, and be bound by the same, and to any and all future changes in or additions thereto, nor to do or suffer any of the acts or things thereby prohibited, and I-we also understand that this Agreement conveys no agency or exclusive-rights of any character whatsoever; and it is expressly understood that I-we hereby agree that in case this Agreement is terminated by the vendor or in case of any violation thereof, or of the Terms or Conditions of sale, the vendor may place and publish my-our name in his removal or suspended list; I-we also agree and execute this Agreement with the distinct understanding that the same is a personal one and not transferable or assignable, and I-we hereby recognize and acknowledge the validity of said re-issued Letters Patent under which licensed motion pictures herein referred to are manufactured and sold.

Signed _Geo K Spoor & Co_

Street and No. _62 n clark st_

City _Chicago_ State _Ills._

Date _Nov 5-08_

Accepted for

SELIG POLYSCOPE COMPANY

By _____

Ben's Kid, *released July 1, 1909, featured Roscoe Arbuckle (l), who would find fame in 1913–15 with Mack Sennett's Keystone as "Fatty" Arbuckle. Roscoe's Selig stay apparently lasted over a year but amounted to little in his career.*

The Heart of a Race Tout, *released July 29, 1909, was the first film made completely in California. Francis Boggs produced it with Jean Ward (fourth from left) and Tom Santschi (center) as stars at the temporary studio on Olive Street between 7th and 8th Streets in downtown Los Angeles.*

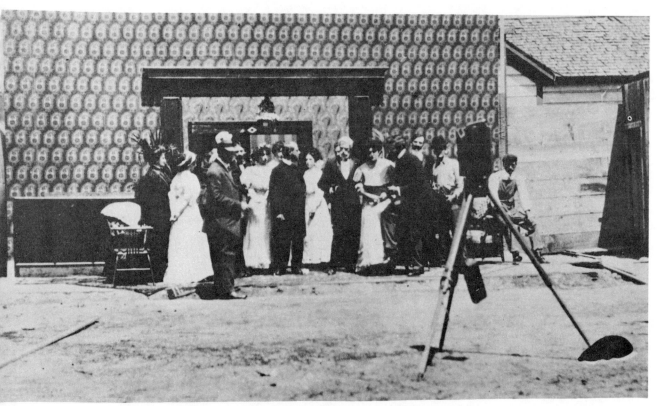

A production shot from the same film, showing cast, director (third from left) and open air set.

*The story of Mrs. Jones Birthday and its companion
subject,* Winning a Widow, *were detailed in this advertising herald of August 30, 1909.*

Supplement No. 170   August 30, 1909

The Hit of the Country---SELIG'S FILMS
Don't Miss These Two on One Reel

Mrs. Jones Birthday

**Released
Aug. 30, '09**

~

Code Word, Day
Length, 540 feet

Winning a Widow

**Released
Aug. 30, '09**

~

Code Word, Widow
Length, 450 feet

THE SELIG POLYSCOPE CO., Inc.
45-47-49 RANDOLPH ST., CHICAGO, ILL., U.S.A.

Mrs. Jones' Birthday

—

Mistakes of the heart do not restrict themselves to single occurrences in a man's life—they often multiply themselves and, moreover, resolve themselves into errors of judgment. So it happened with the sincere but unfortunate Jones.

It was the anniversary of his wife's birth, and she, womanlike, did not fail to impress the fact upon her husband's mind as he departed at his usually early hour for his customary day's work. A bit excited over the prospect of presenting his better half with a gift befitting the occasion, he loses his balance as he steps out of the front door and rolls pell-mell down a flight of six steps to the street. Picking himself up he boards a street car, and arriving at his office he goes through his daily routine of business.

At the close of office hours he repairs to John Post & Co.'s crockery establishment, and after much cogitation and repeated questioning purchases a rather handsome jardiniere. Delighted with his choice and anticipating the caress he will receive in return, he again takes a car, this time for home. As he seats himself he is accosted by an old friend. After a reminiscent talk Jones arrives at his destination and alights, forgetting his jardiniere. The car speeds on. Poor Jones, recovering his wits and realizing that he dare not return home without some token, betakes himself to the same store and purchases another jardiniere.

Again en route to his car, while passing a grocery store, Jones is hailed by another old acquaintance. In the goodfellowship of this accidental meeting, Jones absent-mindedly places his wife's present on the rear end of the grocery wagon near by. Thereupon the driver departs with his wagon and is out of sight before Jones realizes what has occurred. He gives chase, but to no avail. He glances nervously at his watch. Exasperated and overheated he rushes back to the store, and to the amazement of the proprietor purchases his third jardiniere.

This time he is determined to get safely home; no friend shall balk his way. His car is in sight, when his attention is attracted by a heated altercation between a lady and a taxicab driver, she claiming that she is being overcharged. Now Jones was ever of a chivalrous tendency, and, upon being requested to decide the dispute, proceeds to do so, after first placing his precious parcel carefully on the sidewalk near the cab. A few words, and with a satisfied feeling of having accomplished an heroic deed, Jones reaches for his jardiniere, but to his consternation finds that the chauffeur has mistaken it for the property of the occupant of the taxicab, and jardiniere and taxicab were "over the hills and far away."

Half crazed with his repeated misfortunes, he rushes back to the same store. The clerk is dumbfounded at the reappearance of this monomaniac on jardinieres, but sells him another. Poor Jones, his very soul distorted by his anticipated reception of a late arrival home on this eventful day, dashes madly for his car, when he is startled by a woman who clutches him, not fondly, but too strongly, and screams into his ears: "For God's sake, help me: my husband is killing my mother!" Much against his will, unfortunate Mr. Jones is urged into an apartment house.

Inside the house he finds himself battling for life, while he is chased madly around the room by a fiend incarnate, who wields an axe with a dexterity so accurate that Jones decidedly disapproves of accuracy. The woman and her mother flee from the house while he, poor man, makes a hurried departure, smashing his jardiniere and screaming anathemas on all birthdays.

Bruised, tattered and heart-sick he again slowly wends his way to the now so familiar store. "Another of the same kind, please," he meekly requests. He at last gets on a car safely. The car is crowded. A workman enters carrying a package, places it next to that of Jones' jardiniere, and he takes a seat beside our friend. At last Jones reaches his destination, and, grabbing the wrong parcel, alights. He enters his dining-room much relieved, and, inscribing a loving message to his wife, he places it beside what he believes to be his well-earned jardiniere.

Calling Mrs. Jones, he points with pride to his gift. She embraces him fondly after reading his words of affection, truly meant but unfortunately so inappropriate. For as she discloses the article so carefully wrapped, lo and behold! it is a workingman's teapot, black with soot. Poor Mrs. Jones, expectant all day, resents what she considers a practical joke, and belabors her husband with words well nigh unspeakable, and leaves the room, vowing that henceforth he is no husband of hers and that she will return to her mother, never again to be called wife by such as Jones. He, amazed and crestfallen, and disgruntled with the world and himself, swears that birthdays should never exist.

Winning a Widow

Herman Winkle, a tailor, is a bachelor whose nephew, Tom, is in his employ. Benjamin Smart, the keeper of a candy store, is also a bachelor, whose niece, Edna, helps him in his store. Winkle and Smart have their places in the same block and are friends, although both have become smitten by a captivating widow, Mrs. Dasher.

Tom and Edna, seeing much of each other, have fallen in love. The opening scene of the picture shows them seated in a rustic nook "spooning." Edna's uncle comes suddenly upon them and objects to their love making, insisting upon Edna's accompanying him and leaving Tom to his thoughts. Smart sends Winkle a note acquainting him of the spooning he has observed and his objection because of their youth; to all of which Winkle agrees and calls upon Smart, assuring him that he thoroughly agrees with him.

Soon Mrs. Dasher, the widow, strolls by, and is greeted warmly by Smart and presented with a box of bon-bons by him. This his niece observes. Later the widow shows it to Winkle, whom she meets as she passes his store, and Winkle realizes he has a rival. He asks permission to call upon her that afternoon at three, to which she consents. Tom, overhearing it, writes a note to Smart asking him to call that day at three p. m., and signs Mrs. Dasher's name to it. It is delivered to him by Edna, his niece.

Winkle and Smart are soon off to the florist, where they purchase bouquets on the quiet and hasten to the widow's home. followed unobserved by Tom and Edna. Winkle, having arrived first, is declaring his love, when Smart appears with the note, which the widow denies having written. Smart is forced to retire and Winkle obtains her consent to his proposal, and is greatly elated, much to the discomforture of Mr. Smart.

Tom and Edna having observed all this obtain an infant from a nurse girl and leave it in front of the widow's cottage. Tom writes on a card:

"H. Winkle,
"Receive your child from its deserted mother."

This he pins to the baby's clothing. The infant is found by the widow, and the card discovered and read by Smart. Winkle, unconscious of anything, appears and is denounced for his perfidy and deceit. Winkle, dumfounded and crestfallen, rushes from the indignation of Mrs. Dasher. At this turn of events Smart feels there is a chance for him, and taunts Winkle with being a married man. Winkle, while pulling his handkerchief out of his pocket to wipe his troubled brow, drops his pocketbook, which Tom, who appears at that moment, picks up, and, unseen by either of the men, slips into Smart's pocket.

Turning to his uncle, he asks if he has lost anything, and Winkle, upon finding his pocketbook gone, is told by Tom that Smart has it. Whereupon Winkle accuses Smart of having stolen it. The widow appears in time to hear the accusation. Smart says "search me." It is done and the pocketbook found. much to his surprise and that of Mrs. Dasher also. Winkle calls Smart a thief, which so angers him that he knocks Winkle down, and in his indignation tears the collar and shirt from him, and, rushing through the shrubbery, he waves them aloft in his anger and finally stamps them under his feet. With Tom's help Winkle recovers his shirt and makes himself presentable. Smart, still feeling the sting of Winkle's accusation, is out for satisfaction.

He finds Winkle trying to catch his second wind, as it were, and charge him at the point of a pistol with having placed the pocketbook in his (Smart's) pocket himself. He threatens to blow the top of Winkle's head off with a revolver which has no chamber in it; but Smart makes a good bluff with it and Winkle knows nothing different until he secures it and threatens Smart. Mrs. Dasher, fearing a serious turn of affairs, comes upon them. The nurse with the empty baby carriage follows in quest of the infant, and Tom and Edna, who have been looking for her, return the child. The nurse, after declaring that Winkle is not the father, goes on her way with an easy mind.

Tom then admits that he with Edna's help is the culprit—that he signed Mrs. Dasher's name to the note; that he pinned the card to the child's clothing and placed the pocketbook in Smart's pocket, all because both uncles opposed his attachment and Edna's for each other. The widow intercedes in their behalf and the young folks are made happy; while she willingly nestles in Winkle's arms and Smart is left to go back to his store and his candies.

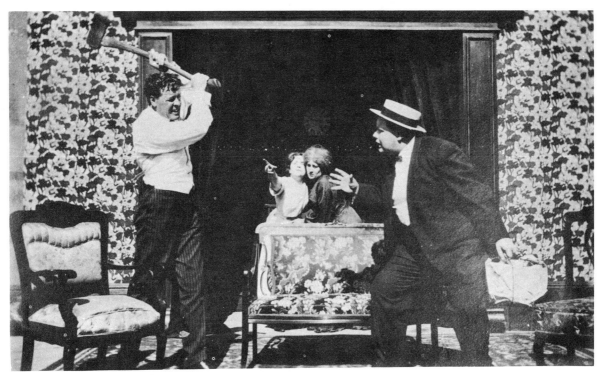

Mrs. Jones Birthday, again featured Arbuckle in a prominent role.

The first set built in Los Angeles on a roof at 8th and Olive for a one-reel version of Carmen. Note the bull-fight poster between the two men, made by cutting the bull from a tobacco carton and pasting it on paper.

A frontal view of the Edendale studio on Allesandro Street shortly after its completion in 1909.

Landscaping and paved streets added to the Edendale facility's charm, circa 1914.

Director Francis Boggs, who was creating a sterling reputation for himself when murdered by a gardener in 1911 at the Edendale studio while in conference with Selig and contractors for the new addition. His place in early film history is a difficult one to evaluate, as only a very few of his films have survived.

An artist's representation of how the Selig Chicago lot would look after construction of the new studio complex (center) in 1911. At the far end of the lot are the stables; note the large artificial lake at center rear around which many of the frontier and Indian dramas were filmed.

The reality in 1911 was somewhat less glamorous; dirt roads and uncompleted landscapes gave it the appearance of a large manufacturing building instead of the magical wellspring of celluloid dreams.

A view of the scenario office, with Editor Kenneth Langly at the front desk; this and the following interior views are of late 1911 vintage.

A corner of the costume department.

The wardrobe room.

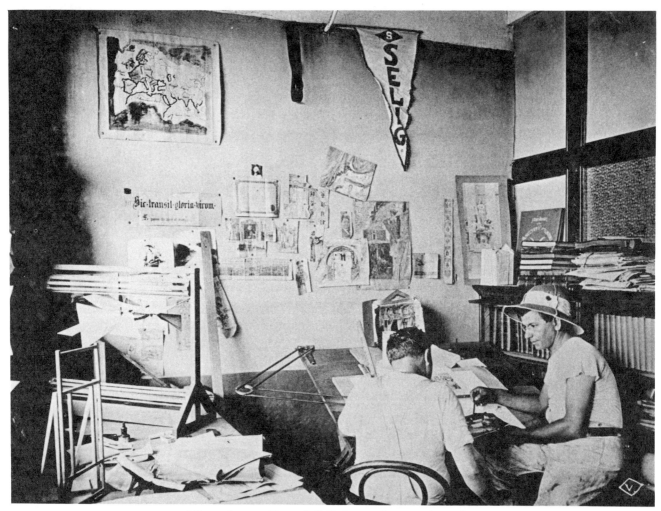

The private office of Selig's scenic superintendent.

A glimpse of the inspecting and finishing room where positive prints were checked and prepared for distribution to exchanges.

Extras awaiting their call on-set in the new studio.

The camera room.

*A corner of the wash room where processed prints
received their final bath before drying.*

A section of the stables.

General offices of the Selig Polyscope Company at 45–49 East Randolph Street, Chicago.

Another view of the Chicago studios after completion of the new building in 1911. The glass building at the left is the original studio erected in 1907.

By 1911, *these advertising throwaways were available for distribution to theatre customers, or for use inside the theatres. A five-color one-sheet at 10 cents was used outside as the "pitch." Note that the throwaway of* Two Orphans *is for the second of three reels only; the film was released on three consecutive days, one reel at a time.*

Kate Claxton's Two Orphans

Selig's Immortal Masterpiece

Produced in Three Reels by Special Arrangement with Miss Kate Claxton (Sole Owner of the Copyright). Staged under Miss Claxton's personal supervision, by Mr. Otis Turner at the Selig Studios, Chicago, U.S.A. All Moving Picture Rights Reserved.

CAST

CHEVALIER MAURICE De VAUDREY ....T. J. Carrigan	PIERRE FROCHARD, The Cripple, His Brother .... James O'Burrell	HENRIETTE ⎰ The Two ⎱ ...... Kathlyn Williams
COUNT DE LINIERES, Minister of Police.....	MARQUIS DE PREALES.......... Rex Rosselli	LOUISE ⎱ Orphans ⎰ ...... Winnifred Greenwood
.... Charles Clary	DOCTOR .... Frank Weed	MARIANNE, An Outcast........ Adrienne Krowell
PICARD, Valet to the Chevalier..... Miles McCarthy	LA FLEUR........................... Will Stowell	LA FROCHARD, The Hag...... Lillian Leighton
JAQUES FROCHARD, An Outlaw · Leighton Stark	ANTOINE.......................... Tom L. Comberford	MADAM GIRARD .... Vera Hamilton
	OFFICER OF THE GUARD..... Louis Fierce	COUNTESS DE LINIERES...... Myrtle Stedman

ENSEMBLE:---Parisioners, Gentlemen and Ladies of the French Nobility, Gendarmes, Soldiers, Peasants, Prisoners, Nuns, etc.

SECOND REEL

T HE COUNT DE LINIERES, now Minister of Police, discovers that there is in existence secret archives containing the histories of noble families. The Countess tells the Chevalier of her early marriage and baby Louise. The Count overhears enough to make him suspicious. The Chevalier tears out the incriminating page and burns it.

The Chevalier, deeply in love with Henriette, arouses the King's displeasure by proposing to the girl. She refuses him and he renews his search for Louise.

Meantime, poor Louise, clad only in rags, is forced to sing on the snow covered streets, by Frochard. Pierre attempts to aid Louise but is rebuffed by Jaques.

The Countess pleads with Henriette not to marry the Chevalier. Henriette hears the voice of her blind sister in the street below, and attempts to rush to her, but is arrested. Louise is dragged away by Frochard.

Miss
Kathlyn
Williams

SELIG

Miss
Winnifred
Greenwood

In the Days of Gold

A Penetrating Analysis of Characters brought out in a Western Story of Thrilling Situations

Written and Produced by HOBART BOSWORTH and F. E. MONTGOMERY

CAST

JUANITA LOPEZ	Betty Harte	JUAN LOPEZ	Frank Richardson
ENRIQUE LOPEZ	Roy Watson	DICK HARDING, *"A black sheep"*	Hobart Bosworth
	MOTHER LOPEZ	Anna Dodge	

THE LOPEZ family is attacked by Indians and are all killed, excepting Juanita and her mother. Juanita hears the shooting, sees the Indians attack her home, and carry off her mother. She decides she would be safer dressed as a boy, so she don's her brother's clothes, and cuts her hair off. Then tries to reach shelter. Dick Harding, a Western cowboy, comes suddenly upon Juanita. She tries to explain to him, but he does not understand Spanish, so she finally makes herself understood by gesticulations. He places her behind him on his horse, and gallops off just as the Indians dash up. After a hard ride, they out-distance the red men and reach camp. The Sheriff, Dick and cowboys pursue the Indians, and come upon them as they are in the act of burning Mother Lopez at the stake. A short fight and the Indians are defeated, but too late, as the mother is already dead.

Harding then takes Juanita to his cabin, thinking she is a boy. They become very much attached to each other. Dick turns miner, and one day makes a lucky strike. Later on he learns that Juanita is a girl and realizing that he loves her induces her to marry him.

Miss Betty Harte

SELIG

Lost in the Jungle

Absolutely the Most Thrilling and Phenominal Animal Picture Ever Produced

Scenario by WM. V. MONG and OTTO BREITKREUTZ.   Produced by OTIS TURNER.

CAST

JAN KRUGA..........Wm. V. Mong	HIRSHAL..........Charles Clary	META KRUGA.....Kathlyn Williams
SIR JOHN MORGAN..Frank Weed	HANS..............Ernest Anderson	"TODDLES".......By Himself

TIME, Present.   PLACE, In the Transvaal.

IN THIS phenominal animal masterpiece, we are told of an incident in the lives of Jan Kruga and his daughter Meta, who live on an isolated farm in the Transvaal.   The nearest neighbor, Sir John Morgan, lives twenty miles away. Toddles, a work elephant on her father's farm, is Meta's only pet, and she constantly defends him from a cruel keeper.   Her father tries to force Meta to marry Hans, a neighbor Boer.   She rebels.   Hirshal, Sir John's nephew, comes for a visit and Sir John brings him to call on the Krugas.   Meta's heart is awakened at the sight of the handsome young Englishman, and she refuses to marry Hans.   For this she is driven away from home by the heartless father and in attempting to walk to Sir John's house she gets lost in the Jungle.   A ferocious leopard attacks her and she defends herself with a hunting knife. She kills the leopard and badly lacerated crawls away. She is found in a dying condition by Toddles, her pet, who has stampeded, and is carried back by him to the farm.   This startling film novelty is filled with intense excitement.   A subject without a parallel in the annals of picturedom.

Miss
Kathlyn
Williams

SELIG

*An artist's representation of the entrance to the Jungle
Zoo. Temporary cages were built on 40 acres belonging to Henry Huntington in 1911. An Italian sculptor,
Carlo Romanelli, came to Los Angeles to work out the
sculpture on-site. Representations of every known
jungle animal made up the frieze encircling the entrance. The Jungle Zoo, completed in 1914 at a cost
of $1 million, became Los Angeles Selig Zoo in 1923
and is no longer in existence.*

2
Making a Selig Film [1]

F. N. SHOREY

Down in the vicinity of Western Avenue and Byron Street, near the exclusive section of Irving Park, Chicago, the inhabitants have become so used to battle scenes and Indian massacres, miniature earthquakes, and mob effects, cowboy feats and Chinese gatherings, that it would take something more bizarre and out of the ordinary than has thus far reached Chicago to surprise them.

They have seen the living counterpart of General Sheridan dashing madly down the road stopping his frightened soldiers in their mad rush from the field of Winchester; they have seen an army of several hundred men in camp and performing all sorts of maneuvers, and have gazed upon twenty or thirty Sioux warriors, some of whom were actually in the famous battle of the Little Big Horn, repeating some of their warlike exploits, so that they may be reproduced by the moving picture machines. In fact, there is little that happens in the neighborhood that surprises them, for they have become used to sensations of this nature.

Down here is a stock company of twelve or fifteen actors, whose names never appear on a program, but whose productions are witnessed by some 300,000 people daily in Chicago, and by as many more in the country towns. In addition, there are regular stage managers, producers, dramatists, and all that goes with a regular theatre. Day by day the stock company meets,

rehearses, and goes through the acts which are prescribed for them by the producer, while their productions are faithfully registered by the machine. But the methods by which the effects are produced which appear so accurately on the canvas in Chicago's numerous moving picture theatres have generally remained a mystery. As a matter of fact, the process is extremely simple. It is mainly the work of the producer, the scenic artist, and the stage carpenter, combined with the work of some clever pantomimist.

For more than a month a band of Sioux Indians, who had never before been off the reservation was encamped down at Irving Park Boulevard and Western Avenue in preparation for the production of a representation of Custer's last fight. Three of the Indians were more than 70 years old, having actually been participants in the tragedy that cost Custer and 300 of his soldiers their lives. Although the Indians were made use of in other scenes, unfavorable weather made it necessary to postpone the battle scene to some other time. While it was impossible to do much outside work, within the big building where most of the productions are staged the company of stock actors is constantly employed.

One day last week a typical war drama was being enacted. The light was good, and the stage had been elaborately prepared. The big room had at one end a painted stockade and guardhouse, and number of men dressed as Confederate and Union soldiers were loitering about. Their make-ups were of the period of 1861,

1. From: *The Film Index*, Vol. IV. No. 5 January 30, 1909, pp. 4–5.

48

and one might have imagined that it was actually that critical time in the history of our country were it not for the conversation of the soldiers themselves, who were conversing on up-to-date topics.

"Get in line, boys," said an elderly man in a gray sweater, who appeared to be the stage director. Half a dozen Union soldiers hastily grabbed as many muskets, and ranged themselves at one side of the stockade. A young man of the hero type becomingly dressed in a Confederate uniform took his place in the midst of the soldiers, while the Union captain placed himself at the head of the men. A young colored boy held a dapple gray horse in position. The Union captain gave a sharp command to his men, who marched briskly several steps forward to the guardhouse. The captain took a hasty glance at the prisoner as the door swung open to admit him, and then wrung his hands.

"My God, I can do nothing," he said in tones of anguish.

"That's the idea exactly, Fred," said the stage director approvingly. "When you get through mount the horse quickly, and you'll have it down fine."

The Union captain being somewhat portly had some difficulty in mounting the horse, but after two or three trials seems to have accomplished it successfully.

"Now start it off again and we'll set the machine to going," said the stage director.

There was a whir and a buzz, the military went through their evolutions again, and another scene had been taken for the benefit of the public.

"You see, this is one scene of a war drama that I got up myself," said the stage director, who was Mr. Otis Turner, formerly with one of Henry W. Savage's companies, and who had also played the original sergeant in Bronson Howard's "Shenandoah." "I expect to call this piece 'Brother Against Brother.' but we don't always know until we see how they turn out. The idea is that the Union captain has taken his own brother prisoner as a spy, and then is compelled to have him shot. I don't know exactly what we'll do with it yet. We may have the Union captain commit suicide rather than shoot his own brother. We'll have to work this out later."

"Do you find this work much different than staging a regular piece?" Mr. Turner was asked.

"I should say I do," he replied. "I found I had to unlearn a great many things when I started in this work, and so do all the actors who take part in it. In the first place, to get an effect with moving pictures there has to be plenty of action. With the average actor repose is one of the strongest methods of obtaining an effect, but it's exactly the opposite here. The gestures have to come quick, and the expression of the features has to change rapidly to convey the idea we wish to. About the first thing we experience with a new actor is his anxiety to write us a great drama. About one experience of it convinces them that they've got a great deal to learn. I think Clyde Fitch or Augustus Thomas would find the same thing if they tried it.

"We get any quantity of manuscripts from would-be dramatists. Some of them are so absolutely absurd that it is astonishing people have the nerve to submit them. This manuscript had for its principal situation a man bound to a piling in the ocean with the tide coming in. Not far from him was his friend, who was bound in such a way that he himself would not be drowned, but would be compelled to witness the drowning struggles of his friend. But one hand is free, and a thought strikes him. He removes his eyeglass, focuses it on the bonds of his friend, the sun burns them through and the man is freed. Now imagine reproducing anything like that as a moving picture. I can't conceive of anything more absurd. And there are scores almost as bad that come to us every day. We don't pay any attention to them, as we find it easier to stage our own plays and write them ourselves."

"You see, it takes quite a knack to become a good moving picture actor," said Fred Herzog, who is the leading man of the company. "I was with the Hopkins company for several seasons with Dave Warfield, Lawrence D'Orsay, Maude Granger, and others. But I found that the things I did on the stage wouldn't do much for a moving picture company. It all depends on the quickness of action and the expression of the features. Everything is different. We don't depend so much on rehearsals as upon our own intuition. We don't always know what kind of a play we are acting in. We just go ahead and do as the stage director suggests and in that way we get our results."

"I believe I like this sort of acting better than I did on the regular stage," said Miss Jean Ward, who is the leading woman of the organization. "I believe I prefer this kind of acting even to Shakespearean roles."

The visit of the Sioux Indians under their Chief Whirlwind was an event long to be remembered on the Northwest side. The three old timers who had actually participated in the Custer fight were variously interrogated, but had little to say regarding it.

"The most we could get from them," said Superintendent Thomas S. Nash of the Selig Polyscope Company, "was that the fight was over so quickly that they could remember little about it. This was about all any of the Indians who were known to have been in the fight had to say. They showed us a good many details about the management of horses that we didn't know before, however."

3
Scientific Nature-Faking[1]

The Roosevelt African Expedition as it was Staged and Photographed for the Stay-at-Home-Man, Nickel to Spend, in a Chicago Moving-Picture Studio Jungle.

The moving-picture companies, whose enterprise ransacks every corner of the earth for graphic subjects to amuse an ever-sated and insatiable public, are already showing "Roosevelt in Africa," a jungle adventure as it was staged in America, the pictures for the film being made in a Chicago studio. A real lion was brought down by the made-up ex-President of the United States, the king of beasts was tied to a long pole and carried to the Roosevelt camp, there hung up and skinned by the glow of the campfire, around which the party gathered.

Preparing the Jungle

The great hunt happened in April, several days before Mr. Roosevelt arrived in Mombasa, Africa, taking place in the studio of a motion-picture company. The lion hunting à la moving-picture plant was far from being free from anger during the time that the movements of the fakers was being recorded by the camera. For, "once a lion, always a lion," and when the fatal shots were fired, Leo came near making the end of the moving-picture Roosevelt and the African beaters otherwise members of Chicago's colored population.

The beginning of the subject, telling of the ex-

President's hunt for big game, displayed the celebrated American and his son Kermit instructing the beaters preparatory to the dash to the jungle. At last, all arrangements having been made, the party was off for a white rhinoceros or anything in the way of an African animal that might turn up.

It was the jungle next—a cage about sixty feet long by twenty wide, with the best jungle scenery that could be manufactured. A bellows was being operated on one side of the cage, giving the effect of a spring breeze, which agitated the bamboo and palms. The cage in which the lion was held a captive was wheeled up to the larger one and the animal admitted to the dense jungle, his native habitation. The creature did not seem to like his new home and became frightened, then bellowed, and, when prodded in the ribs with poles, sought a place to lie down back of all the vines, bushes, and other scenery.

The Home-Made Beaters Earn Their Pay

From the camera platform it was the most realistic thing in the world. Hardly had the lion hidden himself from view when the beaters, headed by the tracker, entered the cage, followed by Mr. Roosevelt and his son Kermit. On all fours, his sharp eyes scanning the

1. From: *Colliers,* Vol. 43, July 3, 1909, p. 13.

ground, the tracker crept forward. At the sight of Leo's fresh tracks, he stopped, bent closer to the ground, then, with effective pantomime, leaped straight up in the air and waved frantically to the rest of the party.

The hunters came forward on the run, Mr. Roosevelt, his son Kermit, and R. J. Cunninghame, the great English hunter of moving-picture make. The hunt was on in real earnest now. The white members of the party retired to the background and a horde of native beaters, stripped to the skin and armed with every conceivable sort of weapon, came forward. The lion again became the center of attraction, and, as the beaters closed in upon him, wilder and wilder he grew. The creature snarled, and it was thought that the crucial moment had now arrived, but, suddenly swirling against one of the beaters, the animal dashed back into the foliage of the jungle. From his present place of hiding the beaters were unable to stir him. There was but one thing to do; desperate action was needed; Mr. Roosevelt must dash into the dense foliage and beard the lion in his own quarters.

Into the Lion's Mouth

The producer bit his lip, and everybody took a long breath. The beaters became scared, but the ex-President was calm, and his eyes rested upon the huge form of the lion. The camera men up on their platform estimated the distance between them and the lion. Not a sound was heard throughout the big studio.

"Are you ready?" the producer asked.

"Ready," replied Mr. Roosevelt, who was then taking aim.

Just as the outdoor American said ready the lion came rushing out of his quarters. The animal did not like the appearance of the man in khaki and came toward him. There was a puff of smoke and the sharp crack of a .303 high-power rifle. The next instant there was a roar such as no lion ever turned loose in a cage, and Leo, his left lower jaw broken by the bullet that went too low, burst out into the open and straight for the men upon the platform. The bars were twelve feet high, but the infuriated animal attempted to jump over them, but fell back, unable to make the distance because of the loss of blood. The sight of blood had now enraged him, and he charged the beaters, but two quick shots, which were not bungles, ended the animal's existence. One of the bullets hit in the right eye

and the other just an inch above. Leo was killed as dead as anything Mr. Roosevelt will bring down in the real Africa. Down on the home-made jungle ground he sank and there passed from the world of moving pictures to the happy hunting ground.

"Get him!" cried the huntsmen, by this time worked up to a stage of real excitement.

The Wounded Monarch Expires

The big native tracker, always on the job, burst through the underbrush and found the slain monarch breathing his last. Again he raised his war-cry and wrapped his arms around his naked body, snake fashion. The other natives hurried up, with Mr. Roosevelt and his son in the lead and the Englishman trailing along beside.

They picked Leo up and looked him over. They counted the bullet holes and shook each other by the hands. Then Kermit wound up the jungle scene by pointing his camera at the natives.

But the realism of Mr. Roosevelt's African expedition did not end here. The game was tied to a long pole and carried to the distant camp. The beaters pranced along gesticulating and shouting. Some natives were passed, including little brown babies.

Night Comes in the Wilds of Africa

"You see, we've got to have the real color in such a picture as this," said the producer at the uncture, "and I believe we've come to as near doing the real thing as it could be done."

Leo, the deceased, was now hung up and skinned. It was night in the wilds of Africa, and the warm glow of the camp-fire reflected on the dark bodies of the natives. While the head tracker and the aforesaid Englishman were engaged in removing the animal's hide, the statesman and hunter, as well as writer, scribbled some notes upon his pad, which probably read:

"Perhaps another century and big-game hunting, as far as lions, elephants, rhinos, and hippopotami are concerned, will be past forever."

This hunt was voted a success. It was considered by the producer the most realistic faking that was ever done.

A Profitable Film

All of the participants in the hunting expedition were pleased with the events of the day, which had been recorded upon hundreds of feet of celluloid. One man who had stood by and watched the proceedings muttered discontent. He was the wild-animal man from whom the moving-picture company purchased the lion.

Although the expense of making this picture was not normal, running well above the $1,000 mark, its total sales will probably net $15,000, and more than one hundred million will enjoy this faking of Roosevelt's African expedition. Many copies of the film were made by the moving-picture company—one hundred and twenty at least—and sent round to the exchanges in the Film Service Association. Each exchange, in turn, will supply the film to the thousands of nickel show-houses that dot the cities and towns.

4
Selig Talks[1]

Mr. William Selig, of the Selig Polyscope Co., of Chicago, Ill., is traveling through Europe. When he landed in London, the reporter of the "Kinematograph & Lantern Weekly" got on his trail and landed him for a good story. Those who know Mr. Selig over here know that he is not much of a talker for publication, but here's what he said to the "Kinematograph" man:

As soon as the "Kinematograph" representative heard that Mr. William Selig had arrived in London and was staying at the Hotel Metropole, the pressman "got right there," to use their own expressive colloquialism. He found the head of the famous Selig Company a typical American gentleman, affable and courteous, but keen all the way.

"I cannot say," he observed, "what my conclusions are as to the picture trade here in England, because you haven't given me time to get around. But I should like to say this, that so far I have been received with the utmost kindness and cordiality in the trade."

"You are one of those who firmly believe that the motion picture has come to stay?"

"Come to stay!" he exclaimed enthusiastically, "why it has only just started. I believe that it will become a permanent feature in the amusements of the public."

"What are you doing over on the other side?"

"Well, we are just putting on the very best films that we can get, in the best appointed theatres we can build. Our object is to educate the people up to the highest class picture entertainment, and we find the response

so quick and so natural as to lead us to conclude that the high-class picture show is a stayer, whereas the lower grade ones will have to go right under."

"Noticing the familiar red cover of the "Kinematograph Weekly" peeping from his pocket, the writer took occasion to congratulate Mr. Selig upon the extraordinary staging effects of the Selig Company's film entitled *Hunting Big Game in Africa,* of which a graphic account appeared in that edition of the "Weekly."

"Yes," said he, "that will show you how earnestly we take the business. We have over in Chicago, in our studio stables, a number of well-trained animals—trained horses, bears, lions, dogs, and even deer. They are all carefully trained to take their part in the making of a film. The whole of that *Big Game Hunting in Africa* was made in our studio, and the lions, the tigers, the elephants, the baboon, and the little lamb were all our own animals trained to 'pose' and to act their parts. Why, we have a horse so well trained that on one occasion a mimic shell accidentally burst beneath it, and the horse just perceptibly flinched, that's all. Our studios and stables in Chicago extend over five acres, and we have another five acres in Los Angeles, where we get our best scenic effects from. We believe in giving the public the most realistic picture we can get, and we're spending a lot of money on it, too. But it will come back," he added reflectively, and with confidence. "I think," he went on, "that we are a long way ahead of you in the equipment of our studios. Of course, I haven't been all around yet—I am going to the Continent when I leave London—but I

1. Reprint of Interview for "Kinematograph & Lantern Weekly" in *The Film Index,* Vol. IV. No. 38 September 18, 1909, p. 12.

haven't met anything yet as good as ours. I have read in your paper the article on Sensational Film Making in Paris, and I want very much to go and see it."

The pressman next referred to the recent struggles between the Moving Picture Patents Company and the Independents, and asked Mr. Selig his opinion.

"Well," he replied, "the Independents can't stand up against the Patents Company, who have made enormous strides, and are now doing better than ever, because they have the command of the best films. The fact is the Independents are financed by the International Projecting Company, who may know something about finance, but nothing about films. The Patents Company was never a trust, and never meant to be. It was simply a business measure of protection and self-help to uphold their patents."

"Do you stand by the home production in the matter of films?"

"Oh, no. When I tell you that seven out of every eighteen reels are European, you will see that we don't. Whatever is best we take—Gaumont's, Pathe's, Urban's are all in great demand."

"And the same with machines; we don't care where they come from so long as they are the best and will project perfectly, and are licensed by the M.P.P. Co. I find," he continued, "that the British-made machine is more highly finished than others, but I don't notice any great difference in the projecting power—given one good maker against another."

In connection with this, Mr. Selig told the writer an incident which shows how acutely the picture business has caught on in America. Over there they advertise the forthcoming films in the daily papers, and the people watch for distinctive makers in the same way as in London the people look for star artists. As soon as they see a Pathe, or an Urban, or a Selig, or some other popular maker, they crowd the theatres just to see those films.

Incidentally, the pressman learned that Americans continue to be great believers in newspaper advertising. It is also the practice in America, the writer gleaned, for the manufacturers to send to the exhibitors, through the exchanges, the story of the film a week in advance. Also in cases where "effects" are used, to have rehearsals before showing. "But effects," said Mr. Selig, "are not a great factor. They are overdone, and the tendency is to spoil the pictures. What we aim at is the perfect picture. Of course, we like a good intelligible story, but we must have the pictures per-

fect. No, we don't encourage vaudeville 'turns' in our best theatres. The price of admission—ten cents—wouldn't allow of the engagement of the best artists, and the mediocre 'turns' have a bad effect on the pictures. Besides, the idea is to build up the picture theatre so that it stands entirely on its own merits. For the same reason we are not very much in love with 'singing or talking pictures.' Unless you have absolutely perfect synchronization the effect is bad and has a tendency to bring the pictures into ridicule. We prefer to rely upon a really good musical accompaniment. At the same time the educated and capable lecturer has an excellent future in the kinematograph industry."

"What is your operator like?"

"I am glad to say we are getting a much better class of men than heretofore. We've known the organ grinder, and still know him; but he is fast being supplanted by a corps of steady, intelligent young electricians who have to pass a board of examiners composed of the municipal electricians in each State. Having once got his license there is no difficulty getting a good situation."

"And I suppose," said the interviewer, "there is also an upward trend in the way of managers of shows. Here in London, there is a marked improvement in the personnel of the manager. The best companies are appointing the educated, tactful, gentlemanly man in preference to the showman, as such."

"Well, the manager does not come into evidence very much in Chicago. You see, in the States the shows are mostly run by individuals, not companies, and each man is his own manager—with the subordinates, of course. We have not gone ahead, like you in England, by the issue of picture stock to the public. We have two and a half millions of people in Chicago with 350 picture theatres, and they are for the most part private enterprise shows. We also have several private companies who own quite a number of theatres. The average seating capacity is between 250 to 300. The prices of admission range from five to ten cents. We are now badly in need of larger theatres to hold between 500 and 1,000 at a cost of from $15,000 to $20,000; with a ten cent to twenty-five cent admission. As to fire precautions since the fearful Iroquois theatre disaster, some five or six years ago, very stringent precautions are insisted upon by the authorities equally in regard to fire-proof theatres and to fire-proof operating boxes and ample exits."

"I have been rather amused to see," continued Mr.

Selig, "that excellently written treatise by Prof. Fred Starr, entitled 'The World Before Your Eyes' put in one of the trade papers here as 'news' and the authorship credited to someone connected with the trade in London. Why, it was written months ago by Prof. Starr, who is one of the leading men in Chicago University, and copyrighted in the States by Mr. George Kleine, Mr. George Spoor and myself."

"Yes," rejoined the interviewer, "it was a very fine bit of writing, and an effective justification—if any were needed—of the raison d'etre of the motion picture show. You, Mr. Selig, have had a strenuous struggle to maintain your patents rights as one of the original promoters of the motion picture."

"Yes, I have been in the business since 1896, and we now rank with Edison and the Biograph Company as the largest manufacturers of films and moving picture machines in America."

As he shook hands the pressman once again endeavored to elicit Mr. Selig's impressions of the trade here.

"No, no," he laughed, "it is too soon to give 'impressions.' I haven't seen enough. I may say, however, in conclusion that if I have an impression at all, it is that your people don't get up early enough."

"Is that to be writ sarcastic?"

"Well," said the head of the famous Selig firm, with a mischievous twinkle in his eye, "I like to leave my hotel at eight in the morning," and with a hearty handshake he was gone.

5

Making "Selig" Pictures[1]

JAMES E. McQUADE

I paid my first visit to the Selig Polyscope Company's plant one day last week, fortified with a note addressed to Thomas S. Nash by Tom Quill, of the publicity department. Mr. Nash is superintendent of the great factory. One can readily conceive that every second of his time has its special value and that to be taken in hand by him from the outset and conducted through all the maze of the mysteries of film making, and have the dark spots in your knowledge thereof illuminated by his simple and lucid explanations is a treasured favor—one that is seldom extended, and not often expected by, a visitor. And let me say here that Tom Nash presides over a democracy out there in the broad acres bounded by Irving Park Boulevard, Claremont and Western Avenues and Byron Street, a democracy in association and good fellowship as breezy and loyal as that which prevailed on the ranges years ago. There is no "Mr." Nash about him. It is "Tom" here and "Tom" there among the host of employees, from the 'ostler up to the producer, for every mother's son and daughter of them knows that "Tom" has his eyes everywhere and that he expects from each a full and enthusiastic measure of service.

Rapid Rise of the Selig Name

Tom Nash has been with Wm. N. Selig since 1897, a year after the business was started. The title of the Company then was the Multoscope & Film Co., which

was retained for a year, being afterwards succeeded by the W. M. Selig Co., which six months later was superseded by the present title, the Selig Polyscope Co.

Those were the days of small beginnings in the old plant at 43 Peck Court, west of Wabash Avenue, near the South Side Elevated railway, when the name of Selig had not even local prominence; but they were also the days of patient effort, of stern endeavor, of the mastery of almost insuperable difficulties, and of optimistic confidence which have given the Selig name international celebrity. Tom Nash started out in life as an electrician, and he changed this occupation for that of a moving picture operator when he first joined the Selig forces. He has followed the destinies of the company ever since, in various capacities, and when the new plant was opened in September, 1907, he took charge as general superintendent.

A Real Dissolving View

To ride out from the busy loop, with over half an hour's travel through noisy streets, and nothing but hurry and scurry and rushing everywhere, and then, suddenly, to be introduced to an outdoor scene in the large and roomy grounds of the Selig manufacturing plant was one of the most vivid transformation scenes that could possibly be witnessed. In a second I was transported to a plain in one of the Dakotas, with U.S. soldiers, officers, civilians, Indians, horses, a fort and frontier houses in view. An Indian girl was just escaping from the second story of the fort by means of

1. From: *The Film Index*, Vol. IV. No. 47 November 20, 1909, pp. 4-6.

knotted sheets and blankets and succeeded in reaching the ground in safety and gaining the back of a horse nearby, while I watched. She then galloped away on the wings of the wind. The guard was prevented just in time, from bringing the earthly career of the red-faced girl to a close by a well directed shot, and, as I changed my position to get the full meaning of it all, I came across the camera man who, under the careful supervision of producer Otis Turner, had been making a negative of the scene which had held me spell bound.

At this juncture, Mr. Nash introduced me to producer Turner, who informed me that they were engaged in making several detail scenes of the Indian War drama, the main scenes of which were taken weeks ago in western South Dakota, in the natural habitat of the Sioux, with real Indians in their war paint and feathers and several companies of U.S. soldiers participating.

"Reels are seldom made in a connected series throughout," said Mr. Turner. "The principal and dominating scenes are first secured amid natural landscape and surroundings, as no artificial scenery photographs with such realism as the natural. And, besides, the perspective and background can best be portrayed from the natural. It is this that makes the truthful depiction of Western drama and spectacles a matter of considerable expense. Now, where it is possible to secure a natural site for operations that is similar to, or will afford surroundings almost like, those in the story of the drama under production, we always take advantage of such facilities. In our reel recently released, which showed a series of fights in the Boer War, I found a section of country, on the Desplaines River, near the Chicago river canal, where the debris and rocks thrown up during excavation afforded an excellent resemblance to the kopjes of the Transvaal. There we acted and caught some of the rough country scenes in that picture."

"And those were remarkably realistic," I interjected, having viewed the film at the Orpheum a few nights before. Where do you get your scenarios?" was the next query.

Selig Producers Write Scenarios

"I write all my own scenarios for the Eastern producing end, and Francis Boggs, an independent producer for the Selig Co., now located on the Pacific

Coast for a year, writes all of his," replied Mr. Turner. Except in two or three cases at the most, we have written all our own scenarios. As you know, we confine ourselves largely to melodramatic subjects, many of these being thrilling war and Indian dramas of Western life; but we also turn out fine spectacles of Western scenery and have made several popular comedies." The foregoing will show that Selig producers have little spare time on their hands. Before passing, it will be pertinent to state that Mr. Turner is a veteran stage director, having no less than an experience of 30 years with first class dramatic organizations to his credit.

Rigorous Censorship of Every Scene

"You can wait until the negative of the scene is developed, and if everything is O.K., you can go for the day," said Mr. Nash to the young lady who had so thrillingly impersonated the fleeing Sioux maiden. The scene had been attempted three times before I had put in an appearance, but it seemed the action of the horse on which she escaped and her manner of getting into the saddle had not been satisfactory to the critical eye of producer Turner. This time it proved all right, and the young lady smiled with a radiance that dispelled the warpaint, showing two rows of pearly teeth and a brilliancy of eye that were fairly captivating.

"She felt sorry for wasting our time and film; but it was not her fault, as the horse was restless from seeing the man lying under the window from which she escaped," said Mr. Turner in explanation.

Large Band of Trained Horses

"Talking about horses, we have the largest and best trained band of horses for this business that you can find in any similar plant in the world," interpolated Mr. Nash at this point. "That is why our war dramas, whether Indian or of other nature, are so signally successful and popular. We can make them lie down, buck, rush away and come back at will. Give them a little exercise, boys," he said, addressing some of the men. And suiting personal action to the command, he himself mounted one of the lithe and supple limbed animals and rode away across the grounds with the abandon and ease of a cowboy. Then to show the perfect control he had of the horse, he succeeded in getting him to lie down without the use of a spur.

The merry pranks and capers of these horsemen and horses was as good as a circus while it lasted. My special attention was directed to old "Rawhide," the bucker. When they want him to "operate" especially well in his stunts, they keep him in stable for a week, without exercise, and then spring him and his antics on some actor who prides himself on his horsemanship. It is said that "Rawhide" has never yet failed to give "Pride" a fall. Then the "clown" horse was pointed out. This comical genius in horse flesh has furnished more amusement than the whole bunch to the field force. A new hand, on attempting to ride him more than a block away from the Selig plant, is puzzled to find that he will persist in turning back homewards. If the rider as stubbornly persists—and he or she usually does—that the "clown" shall continue on in the path ahead, a bit of hair-standing and shivers is the customary result; for the "clown" rears up in a way that threatens a back somersault, with the rider underneath, and a sly, laughing horse is allowed to bear an object and thoroughly tamed man or woman back to the stables. Two 'ostlers are kept busy attending to the horses and stables in the Selig plant.

The New Polyscope Machine

Adjoining the barn and stables is the machine room, well lighted, ventilated and comfortably heated. Here a large force of skilled mechanics is busily employed in manufacturing the new Polyscope projecting machine. All the parts are fashioned here, except the sheet iron framework, and the machines are assembled and thoroughly prepared in this department for the market. It is expected that the new machine will be ready in about 20 or 30 days. Mr. Nash pronounces it a thoroughly up-to-date, and one of the most perfect, projecting machines yet brought out.

Perfectly Equipped Shops and Studio

Space forbids a detailed description of the perfectly equipped carpenter shop, property and wardrobe rooms and the magnificent studio on the grounds, and contiguous to the main manufacturing plant. In the carpenter shop and studio some clever planning and practical mechanical work are done every day. I

noticed a trick bridge that has been built over the large artificial lake, on the west end of the grounds. This is to be used in the near future in the production of a reel that will have a thrilling water scene, in which a horse and his rider will be seen galloping across a bridge, high above the water, when suddenly the structure will collapse in the middle and precipitate both into the flood. The scenic artist and the carpenter combine to produce these effects and both, aided by a large band of assistants, are kept as busy as the proverbial nailer.

In the property room one can find almost any kind of article for use in adding to the realism of a scene, whether oriental or occidental; and besides, the property master is always ready to add an adjunct of any nature that may be called for, at a few hours' notice. Nothing is overlooked to make the Selig film a perfect, true-to-nature subject.

But the studio! A truly magnificent structure is this! Lofty, of extensive ground area, and fully equipped with the most modern appliances and facilities for scenic productions. The roomy space is of such splendid proportions that imposing exterior scenes, which call for over a hundred people and nearly as many horses and other animals, can be put on with ease, and in such manner as to give the effect of a great out-of-doors spectacle. Mr. Pollock, scenic artist and superintendent of the studio, has already accomplished wonders within its glass-fretted walls. In Winter, when the weather prevents the producing of scenes in the open, the studio enables the Selig forces to put on some fairly astonishing out-door scenes, brimful of action and open air realism.

The Making of Film

It must not be forgotten that my fidus Achates, in the shape of Tom Nash, has been diligently accompanying me all this while; and now he is about to initiate me into the mysteries of film making. I must confess that my knowledge was somewhat hazy before he took me under his tutelary wing, and if he was surprised at any time over my ignorance of many things in the fascinating operations—from the inferno of the perforating, printing and developing rooms, with the dull red, cylindrical eye of the presiding demon of those regions as the only source of light that relieved the Egyptian darkness, up to the pleasant finishing room, where bright, intelligent and clear-faced girls first wiped, and then cemented in one continuous whole the various scene-sections of each reel—he never once betrayed himself and was always the ready, patient listener and answerer to every query put to him.

The Negative

In this description, there will be no attempt made to give an abstruse, technical narrative of the various stages in the manufacture of the moving picture that gives so many millions of people delightful and instructive entertainment. The method employed will be rather that followed when one teaches a boy or girl to read; they are first taught to read a sentence and understand its meaning, without any knowledge, whatever, as to its syntactical construction. The latter is best discussed and understood later on.

The film, whether negative or positive, of a moving picture is a thin, semi-transparent, tenacious strip of gelatinous substance, of regular width, somewhat of the appearance of isinglass, though not, like it, scaly, nor as rigid. It is pliant and easily wound on a reel, but it is not elastic. Formerly the substance, from which the film was made, was very inflammable, being of the nature of celluloid. At present the film substance is non-inflammable, a notable step forward, since it provides against the danger of fire.

As in photography, a negative of a picture is first made and from that a photograph, or positive, is printed. The film manufacturer furnishes the manufacturer of moving pictures with negative film strip and positive film strips. The moving picture manufacturer takes this negative film strip, which is carefully kept from exposure to light, into the dark, perforating room, where a machine punches out small, circular holes, at regular intervals, along both edges. This punched strip of negative is wound on a reel and placed in the upper section of the dark chamber of the camera, and is so connected and adjusted with the mechanism of this moving picture camera that, when a handle is turned, the strip of film is unwound from the reel in the upper section of the camera chamber and, passing vertically downwards, is wound on another reel in the lower section of the chamber. Moreover, when the handle turns, it turns a circular metal disc, directly opposite the lens opening of the camera. This circular disc is not complete, a V-like section

being clipped out of it from the circumference to the center. When the handle makes a complete turn, there is a certain space of time during which the V opening leaves exposed to the lens opening a small section of the strip of film.

Suppose the cap is off and the handle is turned, at the time of such exposure, the section of film receives the image of any object in front of it, and if the disc revolves at the rate of 40 times in a second, the film strip traveling downward will record that many images of the objects in front of it. If it be a horse galloping in the line of view for a second, there will be 40 images of his continuous movement shown on the negative film. And thus a whole panorama of objects will be recorded on the negative strip, or a scene occupying many minutes will be imaged, the light being restricted only by the length of the negative strip in the camera chamber.

When a negative of a reel is made it is carefully examined by the producer and if it passes scrutiny it is sent to the developing room, where it is subjected to a chemical bath, thence to the washroom and the drying room, and to the vault, where it is tested by means of a projecting machine and a screen. If it passes this test, the section is placed in an oblong metal box, bearing the number assigned to this particular reel subject, where it is joined by the other sections as fast as they are produced, until the reel story is complete. Any section that fails to stand the projecting test is destroyed and the work of producing must be done over again, even if it takes days and many hundreds of dollars to do it.

Making the Positive Film

Granted, now, that our negative of the reel under attention is all ready and that we require a positive made from it—the film that is used in moving picture theatres. It is reminded the reader at this point that the negative strip of film and the positive strip is made of exactly the same gelatinous substance, the only difference being that the negative is subjected to a certain chemical emulsion, and the positive to another which is different in its properties and action.

The positive strip of film, as was the negative at first, is taken into the perforating room where circular holes are punched along its edges, just as in the negative strip. This perforating room is a thoroughly dark room, that is, there is no white light shown, as are also the printing and developing rooms. After the perforation process, the positive is taken into the printing room, where by ingenious machinery and adjustment it is so placed that it comes in contact with the negative strip in minute sections throughout its whole length. The negative and the positive strips being unwound from their respective reels at the same rate of speed, each passes downwards and is brought in close contact with the other by means of a vertical "clip," in minute sections as referred to. When such contact point is reached, the mechanism is so arranged that a ray of white light enters through an aperture in the wall of the dark printing room, the light being furnished by an incandescent globe in a narrow chamber adjoining the printing room. The light throws the image or scene on the negative strip upon the positive —the negative strip, of course, being nearest the aperture. Thus every image depicted on the negative is impressed, or rather thrown, on the positive and held there.

The positive being printed, it is next taken into the developing room, where it is wound around a large, grooved, thin plate cylinder, which is placed so that when turned on its axis the under surface passes through the developing chemical solution in a trough beneath. This process completed, the strip of film is wound on a large wooden reel and conveyed to the wash room, the reel revolving in a trough of wash water and thoroughly washing the strip for a stated period. The film is then wound on another large wooden reel, brought in from the drying room, to which apartment it is taken and placed in one of the racks provided.

The wash room, dry room, finishing room and vault are supplied with natural light, the temperature of the dry room being kept uniformly at 70 degrees F. This is done by means of a fan which forces air from the outside over the surface of a steam radiator.

The film is next passed to the finishing room where it is first wiped with cloths by nimble fingered girls, section by section—the reader will understand, of course, that the positive comes to the finishing room in scene sections, corresponding to those of the negative. These sections are passed on to other girls who carefully cement them, taking care that the scenes follow each other in proper succession, and as each reel subject is completed it is subjected to the scrutiny of a lady examiner. This examiner has a scene plot of the story of the reel in front of her, as she minutely observes every mark on the film, noting that telegrams, letters, scenes, title, etc., are all in proper place. As she does this, the film is being wound on the metal reel that holds it until marketed and used in some theatre.

Smooth Running of Departments

In the Selig plant these departments are constantly running with the precision of clock work, always keeping in pace with the operations of the producers and their large field forces. The whole machinery, inside and out, is always under the vigilant eye of Tom Nash; and he, in turn, and all his aids, together with the complex business machinery required to market the product and conserve its interests, are held in stable control by the quiet man who hides himself in his office and denies himself to all comers with the pertinacity of a Bismarck—Wm. N. Selig.

The Camera Squad

Far be it from me to overlook the Selig sharp-shooters—the camera squad. Did not one of them, Emmett Vincent O'Neill, cover himself with glory by a display of intrepid courage, during the thrilling lion hunt in Africa, that is still remembered with pride— and laughter! That lion was a grim, fierce cat all right. O'Neill was perched on a platform, above the cane-brake, when the first shot struck the brute in the jaw and put him in a frenzy of passion. The only living object he could see was the camera man, who kept turning the handle of his machine as if it were a gatling gun turned on the foe, and he made a straight rush for him. The lion jumped once for the platform and failed by about two feet; then jumped the second time and missed by barely a foot. The namesake of the Irish patriot did not wait for the third attempt; he did a little jumping himself and landed in a place of safety.

"Why did you jump from the platform when you knew the lion could not reach it by a foot?" asked Tom Nash, after the affair was all over and the lion had become a good Indian.

"Yes, I was perfectly sure the lion could not touch that platform by a foot, perfectly sure," replied O'Neill. "But I remembered that out at home there was a little wife, two pet canaries and a good supper awaiting me and I just thought I wouldn't disappoint them—and I jumped." The other doughty members of the camera squad are Jas. A. Crosby, Hy. Reimers and Thos. A. Persons, whose work on field and plain has gladdened the eyes of millions of moving picture lovers.

6

Pointers on Picture Acting

THE SELIG POLYSCOPE CO.
1910

ACTION.—When the director gives you the word for action at the start of a scene, don't wait and look at the camera to see if it is going. That will be taken care of and started when the action settles down to where the directors think the scene should start.

LOOKING AT THE CAMERA.—Never look toward the director when he speaks to you during the action of a scene and while the camera is running. He may be reminding you that you are out of the picture, or of some piece of business that you have forgotten. Glancing toward the camera near the finish of a scene to see if it has stopped is also a bad habit. The director will inform you when the scene is over.

EYES.—Use your eyes as much as possible in your work. Remember that they express your thoughts more clearly when properly used than gestures or unnatural facial contortions. Do not squint. You will never obtain the results you are striving for if you get into that very bad habit.

MAKING EXITS.—In making an exit through a door, or out of the picture, never slack up just on the edge; use a little more exertion and continue well out of range of the camera. Many scenes have been weakened by such carelessness.

LETTER WRITING.—In writing before the camera, do so naturally. Do not make rapid dashes over the paper. You completely destroy the realism that you are expected to convey by so doing. When reading a letter mentally count five slowly before you show by your expression the effect of the letter upon your mind.

READING LETTER.—When a lady receives a letter from her sweetheart or husband she must not show her joy by kissing it. That is overdone and has become so common by usage in pictures and on the stage as to be tiresome.

KISSING.—When kissing your sweetheart, husband or wife, do so naturally—not a peck on the lips and a quick break-a-way. Also use judgment in the length of your kiss. Vary it by the degree of friendship, or love, that you are expected to convey.

GESTURES.—Do not use unnecessary gestures. Repose in your acting is of more value. A gesture well directed can convey a great deal, while too many may detract from the realism of your work.

STRUGGLING.—Avoid unnecessary struggling and body contortions. Many scenes appear ridiculous by such action. For example, if in a scrimmage you are overpowered by superior numbers, don't kick, fight and squirm, unless you are portraying a maniac or a man maddened beyond control. Use common sense in this.

SHUTTING THE DOORS.—Be careful in opening and shutting of doors in a set, so as not to jar the scenery. Carelessness in this respect causes make-overs, with a considerable loss of time and film, both of which are valuable.

IN PICTURE.—Be sure that you stay in the picture while working. Mentally mark with your eyes the limitations of the camera's focus, and keep within bounds. You can do this with a little practice and without appearing purposely to do so.

SMOKING.—Don't smoke near the camera or where

the smoke can blow across the lens. Take just as good care about kicking up a dust. If you are on a horse it is not necessary to ride circles around the camera. Throwing dust into a camera will cause scratches, and bring down upon your head the righteous wrath of the operator.

GOSSIP.—Avoid discussing the secrets of the business you are engaged in. Remember that much harm is done by spreading the news of all the happenings of the day in your work. Revealing to outsiders the plots and names of pictures you are working on or have just finished is frequently taken advantage of and causes great loss to your firm, by some rival concern rushing a picture out ahead that they have on hand, of the same nature. All gossip of an injurious nature is deplorable, and will not be indulged in by any people who appreciate their position and wish to remain in the good graces of their employer.

PROMPTNESS.—Come to work on time. An allowance of ten minutes will be granted for a difference in watches, but be sure it is ten minutes BEFORE and not ten AFTER. There are no hardships inflicted upon you, and you owe it to your employer to be as prompt in this matter as you expect him to be in the payment of your salary.

MAKE-UP.—Regarding make-up and dress, do some thinking for yourself. Remember that the director has many troubles, and his people should lighten his burden in this matter as much as possible. For example: If you are told to play as a "49" miner, figure out in your own mind how you should appear, and don't ask the director if high-laced boots will do when you should know that they have only been in use for a few years. Don't ask him if pants with side pockets will do, when you know they were never worn at that period. A poor country girl should never wear high French heels, silk stockings and long form corsets; nor should her hair be done in the latest fashion. She would look very much out of the picture in such a make-up carrying a milk pail. Do not redden the lips too much, as a dark red takes nearly black. Likewise in rouging the face, do not touch up the cheeks only and leave the nose and forehead white. The effect of such a make-up is hideous in photography.

Get in the habit of thinking out for yourself all the little details that go to complete a perfect picture of the character you are to portray. Then, if there is anything you do not understand do not be afraid to ask the director.

BEARDS.—In the making of beards one cannot be too careful. This is an art that every actor can become proficient in, if he will only take the pains to do so. Remember that the camera magnifies every defect in your make-up. Just use your mental faculties to give some thought to your character studies and you will win out.

SLEEVES.—Avoid playing too many parts with your sleeves rolled up. Cowboys and miners use the sleeves of their shirts for what they were intended. If you are playing tennis, or courting a girl at the seaside, you may display your manly beauty to your heart's content. Do not let common stage usages govern you in this matter.

PROFANITY.—Let the gentlemen exercise care when in the presence of ladies and children to use no profanity. It is just as easy to express yourself without it if you will only try it.

USE NO PROFANITY IN THE PICTURES.—There are thousands of deaf mutes who attend the theatres and who understand every movement of your lips.

PARTS.—Do not become peeved if you are not given the part you think you ought to have. The director knows what type of person he wishes to use in a particular part, and if it is not given to you it is because some other person is better fitted for it.

We should all work for the general good. By giving our employer the best we have in us, we are greatly benefiting him, and by so doing are enhancing our own value.

The Roman. *Betty Harte, Hobart Bosworth, Robert Leonard. February 24, 1910. Leonard later became a well-known director.*

The Code of Honor. *Al E. Garcia and Frank Clark.*
March 13, 1911.

The Cowboy and the Shrew. *Herbert Rawlinson. April*
10, 1911. ½ reel.

The Witch of the Everglades. *Kathlyn Williams. April 27, 1911. Produced in Florida by Otis Turner.*

Back to the Primitive. *Charles Clary, Kathlyn Williams, Joseph Girard. May 11, 1911. Produced in Florida by Otis Turner.*

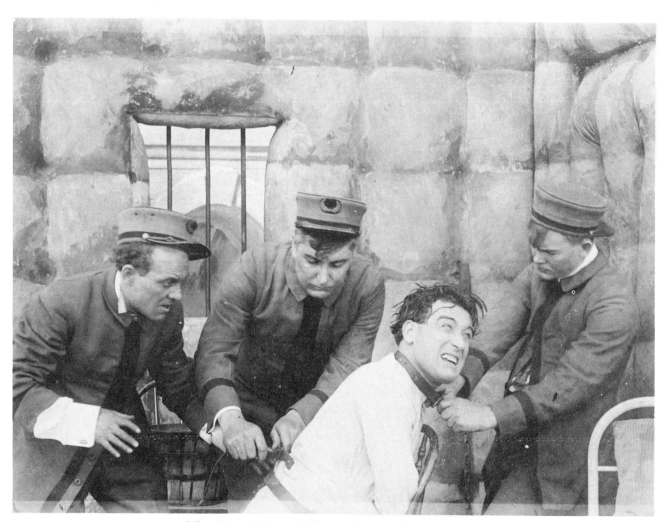

The New Editor. *William Duncan. June 29, 1911.*

Their Only Son. *Al E. Garcia and Nick Cogley.*
August 10, 1911.

The Blacksmith's Son. *Anna Dodge, Tom Santschi,*
Betty Harte. August 17, 1911.

Saved from the Snow. *Bessie Eyton. August 21, 1911.*

In the Shadow of the Pines. *Lillian Hayward, Bessie Eyton, Herbert Rawlinson. August 28, 1911.*

The Heart of John Barlow. *Tom Santschi, Baby Lillian Wade, Betty Harte. September 8, 1911.*

Making a Man of Him. *Herbert Rawlinson, Betty Harte. October 16, 1911.*

The New Superintendent. *Herbert Rawlinson, Nick Cogley. November 16, 1911. Hoot Gibson can be seen behind Rawlinson.*

The Little Widow. *Herbert Rawlinson and Betty Harte. December 22, 1911.*

7

The Wonders of a Picture Factory[1]

Even the exhibitor who makes his living by and devotes the best part of his life to the showing of motion pictures to the public has usually a very vague conception of the way in which the pictures are made. Of course he knows in a general way that the actors must be trained in their work, that money must be spent for costumes, scenery and properties, that each scene must be rehearsed a number of times before it is taken by the camera. He may even, if he is sophisticated, be able to trace the whole course of the photoplay, from the brain of the scenario writer to the screen, without missing a detail. But he cannot know, until he has seen, the vastness of the modern picture plant—the wonders of its accumulation of properties and its provision for every possible requirement.

Our leading story this month is a description of the Selig factory in Chicago. We have selected Selig as the victim because his plant is in many respects unique, while at the same time it is typical of the bigness of the business. It is a fine example of the lengths to which those broad, big men who have made the business what it is will carry their faith and enthusiasm.

People talk, sometimes, of the ephemeral nature of the photoplay. Is there anything ephemeral about a million dollar plant, built to last forever? Who is a better judge of the stability of a business than the man who has grown up with it, and for whom it has made a fortune from nothing? Mr. Selig's faith in motion pictures might betoken either good judgment or an overcharge of optimism. But it takes more than optimism to make a fortune out of any business.

Men of the trade who have attained wealth or position are generally regarded as lucky because fate threw them into the irresistible rising tide of a phenomenal business. The Selig history shows none of the influence of "luck," however. Selig and his plant have prospered, and prospered amazingly, in spite of early hardships and possible blunders, but it was foresight, and judgment, and nerve, and enthusiasm, and above all hard work that did it. The Selig personality is ample proof of that. Those who depend on luck grow arrogant as they prosper. Those who achieve grow even kindlier and more appreciative of their employes and associates as success comes. And W. N. Selig is a veritable idol of his associates. Not one of them but believes the Selig plant the greatest, the "Diamond S" pictures the finest, and W. N. himself the best, in the world.

With such assistance, or call it, rather, co-operation, with such a spirit, the Diamond S will be capable of even greater things than it has yet accomplished. Its greatest handicap, paradoxically, has been rapid growth and the constant demand for more space and faster work. There is plenty of room now that the new studio is finished. Private offices and a library are at the disposal of the producers. The property stores yield means to materialize any idea whatsoever, no matter how bizarre or even grotesque it may be. The people of the stock are provided with every comfort and convenience. In a word, conditions are ideal for the production of perfect pictures.

1. An editorial which introduces the following article in *Motography*, Vol. VI. No. 1, July, 1911, p. 3.

Familiarity breeds contempt, and the things that are most commonplace to the Selig forces would seem strangest to the layman. Camels grazing in vacant lots, red Indians pursuing bears across a little lake, or wolves swimming after deer in the same pool of water—these are almost of everyday occurrence and indicate merely the rehearsing of some of those magnificent animal or jungle pictures for which the Diamond S has become famous. Splendid specimens of strange beasts are as common at the Selig plant as they are in any big circus.

With due regard for the immensity of the Selig property, the greatest moral to be drawn from its inspection lies in the realization that it is only one of many. Selig's product, voluminous as it is, supplies probably less than one-sixteenth of the country's demand. How vast a field are we occupied in, and how great are its future possibilities! The producer who today is amusing the pleasure-seeking public with light drama tomorrow will make the pictorial textbooks of a nation's schools; while the entertainment feature, developed as literature is now developed, will have its own Rudyard Kiplings and Mark Twains. Credit and publicity for the scenario writer and the producer will inevitably improve the quality of plots and attract better talent into the field. Observant ones will notice that Selig, for one, is giving that kind of publicity in his bulletins. It is only another step to put the names on the film.

Our story of one big motion picture plant, inadequate as the description is, should serve to awaken in the exhibitor a sense of stability and permanency of his business, and in the layman a greater respect for the evening's entertainment he views so lightly.

Wonders of the Diamond-S Plant[2]
EUGENE DENGLER

If you take the Irving Park Boulevard car in Chicago and travel toward Western Avenue you will presently see, a little ways off to the south, a group of buildings, chimneys, and various queer-looking structures, scattered over several acres of ground, and all surrounded by a high board fence. The tallest and most commanding member of the group is a building some four or five stories high, with a peaked roof, all of

2. From: *Motography*, Vol. VI. No. 1, July, 1911, pp. 7-19.

glass, looking like some large and lofty greenhouse. You immediately wonder what they are raising up there, and your curiosity is more augmented than satisfied when somebody replies that they are "raising" motion pictures—that this whole fence-enclosed domain is a motion picture plant. Then you notice somewhere the sign "Selig Polyscope Company"—it is emblazoned in several places—and you realize that this is the home and breeding ground of Selig photoplays. Then you understand a thing that has puzzled you all the time—those queer low structures just raising their heads above the fence, which from one angle look like the tops of mountains, castles, towers, and houses, and from another just plain piles of canvas and lath. You realize that these are open air settings for film plays. Of course you want to go right in and look around.

You enter by the main office, which is on the first floor of the large building with the glass roof—the studio; it is a spacious, airy, tastefully decorated room where the administrative ends of the business are brought to a center. Mr. Selig's private office is off to the left, and in this outer room sit several of his lieutenants. There is a private branch exchange telephone switchboard near the door; an elaborate time-clock system with pockets for four hundred employes against one wall; various desks, some for clerks and some for bosses; and the regulation drinking stand with its inverted jar of filtered water. So far the place looks like any busy industrial establishment.

Not until you mount to the second story do you begin to breathe the atmosphere of stage-life and theatricalism. The whole second floor is given over to the producers, actors and camera men. Each of the producers, Otis Turner, Joseph Golden and William V. Mong, has a private office, and there is a library for their use in common. Here they plan and write their scenarios, each producing at least one a week, and sometimes two. These men are skilled by long experience in their line of work, having graduated from service on the legitimate stage. Otis Turner, a veteran of stage directing, served twenty-five years with Savage, Jacob Litt and Frohman prior to his connection with Selig. Kindly, genial, and unassuming when off duty, Mr. Turner is in action a whirlwind commander —a veritable Napoleon in handling difficult scenes and large groups of actors. His attention seems to be everywhere at once, commanding, urging, suggesting, coaxing, cajoling—a human embodiment of omniscience and omnipresence. Such films as "The Two Orphans," "Rose of Old St. Augustine," "Back to the Primitive," "Captain Kate," and those wonderful Boer war dramas taken at Willow Springs, Ill., where 250 actors under military discipline performed before the camera, are Otis Turner's special province. A conversation with Mr. Turner when he dips into the stores of his comprehensive experience is an education. He is a firm believer in the uplift of the business, and bases large hopes on the rapid advancement of the past two or three years. Like all the progressive producers, he is crying for new and better ideas, and believes that publicly crediting film plays to their authors will result in better scenarios. The Selig company, by the way, will soon inaugurate this practice .

Joseph Golden, like Otis Turner, is a stage director with many years of experience behind him. His first training was gained with Dion Boucicault over twenty years ago. Later with Charles Frohman and other leading managers his skill grew to maturity. An author, an actor, a playwright, Mr. Golden has drunk deep at all the wells of culture that go to supply the mental resources of the perfect producer. He is one of the most prolific writers of scenarios in the motion-picture business, generally producing film plays of his own authorship. Mr. Golden has an abiding faith in the artistic and educational possibilities of the motion-picture business, and his policy is one of "uplift" at all times.

William V. Mong is a recent addition to the Selig producing staff. His ability may be judged by a picture, entitled "The Way of the Eskimo," soon to be released by Selig. It is a remarkable picture laid in the land of eternal ice, the majority of the actors being Eskimos. There is a dramatic plot, but the chief interest will undoubtedly lie in the many strange customs and ceremonies bound up with the life portrayed. The film reflects great credit upon Mr. Mong's directing ability.

The Selig producers receive many scenarios from outside sources. They have used adaptations of Henry K. Webster, Frank L. Baum, C. E. Nixon, Rex Beach and Elbert Hubbard stories, as well as good stories from unknown writers. Manuscripts that contain the germ of a good picture play are accepted and paid for. Then they are whipped into shape for production before the camera by one of the Selig producers.

Few troupes of actors in this country are accorded as many comforts as the Selig stock company. Commodious individual dressing rooms, shower baths, a large green room, smoking and card room for the men, a sitting room for the ladies, are some of the things provided. In fact, the actors' quarters have much the atmosphere of a club. For the super-numeraries, who are sometimes employed by the score, there are large sanitary dressing rooms, offering all the modern conveniences.

Adjoining the actors' quarters is the wardrobe room where the components of 7,000 costumes are kept in stock. The catalogue of this immense aggregation of wearing apparel reads like a table of history, for there is no period or clime whose costume lacks representation. Every style of costume, from the fig-leaf to the hobble-skirt, can be brought forth at a moment's notice. A large assortment of wigs is also included.

On the third floor is the studio proper, an enormous room, 179 by 80 feet, whose solid glass walls and roof rise two and a half stories above the floor. Needless to say the light of day flows in here unimpeded. One would expect the place to be a very hot hot-house, but such is not the case. One finds instead that the atmosphere is remarkably fresh and cool. This is due to the fact that filtered and refrigerated air is forced up from the basement through large ventilating funnels such as are seen on ships. On the sultriest day one will find the enormous room airy and refreshing.

A feature of the studio is a large elevator with platform dimensions of approximately 10 by 20 feet, which is used to hoist heavy properties and scenery painted in another part of the plant. It is a monster elevator, looking large enough to carry a house; but it is dwarfed to a moderate perspective by the proportions of the gigantic room in one corner of which it finds a place.

Frequently three scenes are in more or less simultaneous operation on the floor of the studio, but this by no means exhausts the space. There is room, one would estimate, for six or eight settings. The interior work is done mainly in the studio, and the exterior work out in the yard, whither we will now repair.

The yard is the most fascinating part of the Selig plant. Here in a large area covering two or three acres the exterior settings are built and set in place. You will see castles, log cabins, bridges, waterfalls, mountains, block houses, palisades, stores, saloons, cottages, and what not, all scattered about the yard, hit or miss, but all facing the southern sun, ready to serve as backgrounds for whatever dramas may be in making at the time. In walking about this open-air curiosity shop you are apt to run onto an ancient sea-going hack, a warlike cannon, an aeroplane, an Indian tepee, a camel, an elephant, a jackass, a flock of geese—almost anything, in fact. You touch elbows with an Indian actor clad in war paint, a Western bad man, an African hunter, a Tennessee feudist, a cowboy girl, a country lass, and many other types of American or foreign humanity. Some of them are formidable personages indeed, but only under the eye of the camera. Engage them in conversation and you will find that their cordial affability belies their make-up.

In the yard is a large artificial pool of some 60,000 gallons capacity. About this pool many beautiful scenes are set, and many spectacular actions take place. The pool forms the setting of several of Selig's remarkable animal pictures. It is here where the wolves swim in pursuit of the deer, and where the intrepid Indian hunter dives after the swimming bear. When you see these scenes on the film you will swear that nothing but nature could have produced them.

A list of actors in the Selig stock companies is here appended. The list does not pretend to be complete, but enough are given to indicate the magnitude of the acting forces:

Count Alberti	Lillian Leighton
Sydney Ayres	Baby Lillian (Wade)
Eugenie Besserer	James L. McGee
True Boardman	Tom Mix
Hobart Bosworth	J. A. Philbrook
Thomas Carrigan	Leo Pierson
Frank Clark	Herbert Rawlinson
Charles Clary	Frank Richardson
Nicholas Cogley	Rex de Rosselli
George Cox	Thomas Santschi
Elaine Davis	Iva Sheppard
Anna Dodge	Marshall Stedman
Tom Duncan	Myrtle Stedman
Virginia Eames	Olive Stokes
Bessie Eyton	W. H. Stowell
Frank Garcia	Otis B. Thayer
Winnifred Greenwood	Stan Twist
Betty Harte	Roy Watson
George Hernandez	Frank Weed
Fred Huntly	Kathlyn Williams
Adrienne Kroell	

In this list many film favorites will be noted. There is Kathlyn Williams, the beautiful and fearless actress who has won much popularity with Selig films in the past and is destined to win even more through her participation in a series of spectacular jungle pictures which Selig is about to release. Miss Williams

says "In this work it is early to bed and early to rise and we certainly are healthier, wealthier and wiser. The work is absolutely fascinating; there is change all the time. Each picture means a new character, and each character is created by one's self. No following in the footsteps of the actor or actress who created the part. If you have the right conception of the part, the producer is only too glad to give your imagination full sway, but woe unto him who thinks he knows it all! One's first picture will take more egotism out of one than all the critics; the actor sees himself as others see him and is quite willing to acknowledge that the producer knows what he is talking about and knows what he wants. The opportunity to improve one's self is limitless! What more can you want than to see yourself act! Then the different characters one portrays! There are characters I have always wanted to try. I could be in stock for years and never have the opportunity to play but one line. In motion pictures one tries them all."

Miss Williams' enthusiasm for the motion picture work is echoed by seemingly all the actors at the Selig plant. Comparing them with their confreres who stick to the "legit" one agrees with Miss Williams that they are "healthier, wealthier and wiser."

Hobart Bosworth, the well-known leading man of the Western stock company, was born in Marietta, Ohio, which, to quote him, was his misfortune and not his fault. He proceeded to remedy this ten years later by running away to sea. He sailed in the American merchant marine for three years, coming ashore in San Francisco, where he boxed and wrestled for a living, and had six months on a ranch in Lower California. He made his first appearance on the stage with the celebrated McKee Rankin stock company in 1885. After the usual diversified experiences of young actors, which included a trip through Mexico with Herman the Great, and several "strandings" of a more or less tragic nature, he became a member of Augustin Daly's company, and remained with that great manager for ten years. Upon the expiration of this long sentence he emerged as a leading man for Julia Marlowe, afterwards playing stock leads in St. Louis and Cincinnati. In 1900 his health broke down and for many years it proved a constant menace, although at different times he played leads with Amelia Bingham, Henrietta Crosman, and was featured by Mrs. Fiske in the initial New York production of "Martha of the Lowlands," and finished the season with Mrs. Fiske, playing Judas, in "Mary of Magdala," Lovborg, Alec D'Uberville, and other leading parts of her repertoire. This season proved too hard, and at its expiration he spent two years in Arizona trying to recuperate, which he seems to have accomplished most thoroughly. In 1907, after a few weeks of special work as leading man, he joined the Belasco stock company in Los Angeles, and remained there until the theater changed hands, acting occasionally. In the spring of 1910 he acted in a special picture for Mr. Boggs, manager of the Western branch of the Selig company, and realizing that the outdoor work of the moving picture was the one method open to him, for reconciling his theatrical knowledge with the necessities of his regimen, he became a regular member of the company, and as the months have rolled on he has found it so fascinating and beneficial to his health, that he is now thoroughly wedded to it. His old athletic life of boxing, wrestling, fencing, riding, sailing, swimming, canoeing and hunting in the snows of the Canadian woods have fitted him to rather an unusual degree for the somewhat strenuous work of the moving-picture actor, and gives him a larger range of subjects than usually obtains.

In addition to portraying leading roles with the Selig company, Mr. Bosworth has written and produced many splendid film productions. Notable among these may be mentioned "The Curse of the Redman," "The Medallion," "The Bargeman of Holland," "Ramona's Father," and "The Code of Honor." During the past few weeks Mr. Bosworth has been engaged in producing mountain stories dealing with the early days of California, using the great Yosemite Valley, clad in its gorgeous winter coat of snow, for the backgrounds.

A recent addition to the Selig eastern stock company is Miss Winnifred Greenwood, a beautiful and charming actress of great talent whose popularity is destined to be unbounded, if the prophecies of those familiar with her recent work may be listened to. The public itself will judge of Miss Greenwood's ability as demonstrated in "The Two Orphans," and "The Tale of a Soldier's Ring," films soon to be released. As the blind sister in "The Two Orphans" her work is characterized by wonderful sweetness and pathos. Her assumption of the leading role in "The Tale of a Soldier's Ring" is most moving and poetic. Any role taken by Miss Greenwood is enhanced on the pictorial side by her great personal beauty. When asked for a few details regarding her stage career, Miss Greenwood replied as follows:

"I was born in Geneseo, N.Y., a very picturesque little place situated in the Genesee valley. What year did you say? Oh, I don't mind telling you. It will be a few years yet before I hesitate on that point. I was born on the morning of January 1st, 1885. My parents were non-professionals, and for that matter, I am the first to initiate the theatrical profession into our family. My first appearance, also my first part on any stage, occurred when I was the age of three years, as little "Leah" in the play of "Leah, the Forsaken." It was in the little town of Towanda, Pa., that I made my wonderful debut, my father allowing me to be the substitute of the little company girl, who was ill. A great many times after that I substituted (to use my mother's expression) with traveling companies who needed the services of a child. I just loved the theater. I thought all the people, the lights, the scenery, the acting, was so beautiful, and I am of the same opinion still. I think acting from an artistic standpoint is wonderful. Oh, of course, not all acting, just the good. I would go to a show, and just yearn to "belong," never dreaming I would be a part of the world I love so dearly. I was sent to boarding school at the age of eight years, having had two years' previous schooling in a private kindergarten at home. Well, as soon as I was able, I started out in vaudeville, my mother traveling with me. Yes, my mother traveled with me until she died. My education did not lack much; my mother being a college graduate, she continued with my education. I remained in vaudeville three years, then drifted into musical comedy. Then I tried dramatic work and I liked that best. I have been in stock eight years, playing in a few of the principal cities of the United States and Canada.

"How long have I been playing leading business? About six years. No, that is not long. Oh, but I worked so hard and studiously to attain that which seemed to me once such a great height!"

"How do I like the motion-picture work? Immensely! Of course, I have had very little experience as yet, but from my limited knowledge, the moving picture artist has as large a scope as any in the theatrical field to improve himself or herself, and also to "uplift" the profession, which the majority of us are anxious to do. I predict a grand, glorious future for the moving picture world and in time it will be universally recognized as belonging to the 'legitimate.' "

A popular member of the western company is Miss Betty Harte. She will be remembered for her work in an innumerable series of pictures in which she took the part of a boy—not a girly boy, but a real boy. Endowed by nature with a slender form, lithe limbs, a boyish face and frank, unabashed manner, she is well equipped for such roles and plays them with great spirit. Dressed as cowboy girl or society heroine, she is equally good—a versatile actress indeed. She now claims California as her home, but was born and reared in Pennsylvania. Her first notion of acting was acquired in private theatricals in which she always took a prominent part. After graduating from a Quaker boarding school she took a course in stenography and for a short time played the typewriter in an office, but this did not appeal. A desire to earn more money, coupled with her ambition to shine behind the footlights, caused her to resign her office position and seek the stage door. She found it at the Girard Avenue Theater in Philadelphia and remained in stock in that city for almost three years. Then a season in vaudeville on the Keith and Proctor circuit ended her stage life in the east. The health of her mother necessitated a change, and they decided to go to California. Her first coast experience was with May Mannery, playing the artist's model in "The Devil." At the close of that season she determined to have a company of her own, and they started out with two plays. Towns were well billed and her hopes were high, but on the second night the leading man "broke up the show" by becoming intoxicated, and she closed the next day, a short and sorry experience, as her own manager. Then Los Angeles and moving pictures. She secured an engagement with the Selig company in August, 1909, and with playing ingenue and many leads she has been a busy lady ever since and likes the work immensely.

Charles Clary, leading man of the eastern stock company, takes pride in claiming Illinois as his home, having been born in the quiet little village of Charleston. Stage ambitions filled him at an early age, and his first experience was gained in amateur theatricals. "In those days," says Mr. Clary, "my ambitions were to be able to blow the living daylights out of a horn, and wear a red uniform with brass buttons and kick up all the dust from Charleston depot to the town 'opery house.' Of course, I would have perhaps considered an engagement with Bernhardt, Nat Goodwin, or Lew Dockstader. Finally luck favored me, and I was taken on by the Burbank stock company in Los Angeles, and later in Portland, Seattle, and Spokane. Then the call of the road seized me with a rheumatic trip, and I found my pay envelope read 'from "The Road to Yesterday" company.' Later 'Glorious Betsy' claimed my attention. Then I became leading man for Mrs. Leslie Carter. During the summer vacation that followed I paid a visit to some friends who were in the Selig company. At once the 'canned drama' appealed to me like getting money from home and I fell a willing victim, and have indeed been very happy in my decision. Two years have now passed and only pleasant memories are recorded with my experience." Mr. Clary's popularity is attested by the voluminous number of messages he receives from admirers among the fair sex.

Surely one of the most adventurous careers which ever found its way into the motion picture profession is that experienced by Miss Eugenie Besserer, one of the leading women of the Selig western company. Miss Besserer was born in Paris, France, but early taken to Ottawa, Canada, where at a tender age she was left an orphan and placed in a convent. Irked by the convent restraint, she ran away when only twelve years old. She found herself in the Grand Central Station, New York with but twenty-five cents in her purse. A street-car conductor assisted her in locating a former governess, whose name only she remembered. Through her she discovered an uncle, at whose home she took up her abode. When fourteen years old Miss Besserer took fencing from Prof. Senac, the world's champion, and became wonderfully proficient. For several years she enjoyed the woman's championship, and many a lively bout she had with Alexander Salvini. Her first theatrical experience with with McKee Rankin and Nance O'Neil. Then followed engagements with Wilton Lackaye, Frank Keenan, a season with the Pike Stock of Cincinnati. She also played opposite Henry J. Kolker for a season. Leaving the stage she returned to fencing and was instructor at Madame Thurber's and the Berkeley Lyceum, Alice Roosevelt being one of her pupils. After four years of teaching Miss Besserer returned to the stage, playing emotional parts, and it was not long before her ability was recognized and she was selected to accompany Margaret Anglin as understudy on her Australian tour. At eighteen she had written a successful play in which she was starred. She also wrote the fencing playlet "An Accident." The illness of her sister took her to Los Angeles, where she became acquainted with the moving picture business, and desiring to remain on the coast, she decided to try her luck in pictures. She is delighted with the work and expects to remain in it indefinitely.

Miss Besserer is especially adapted to the work, as she rides and swims as well as fences.

While on the subject of Selig actors, mention certainly must be given to the troupe of animal actors which form one of the most interesting features of the entire establishment. There are 12 lions, 9 cub lions, 1 elephant, 3 camels, 10 leopards, 7 leopard cubs, 5 pumas, 1 monkey, 3 bears, 2 deer, 10 eskimo dogs, 8 grey wolves, not to mention mules, geese, dogs, horses, etc. This menagerie gives the Selig plant a distinct character among the places of its kind, and has enabled it to lead all others in the production of animal stories, or what might be termed the drama of the jungle. Lions growling in the path of a heroine alone in the wilderness, a blood-thirsty leopard leaping upon the prostrate form of the same heroine, a battle royal between two leopards and a lioness, the tracking of two deer by a pack of hungry wolves—these are some of the elements that are interwoven into picture dramas throbbing with life and human interest. The plays of this character already released by the Selig company ("Back to the Primitive" will be remembered as one of them) are but forerunners of many more which were staged in the Florida jungle last winter, and others which are now in the process of making at the Chicago plant. Will they make a hit, these pictures? They undoubtedly will, for they combine sensation and novelty in the highest degree, two qualities for which the public has always shown a liking. They recall those animal games and contests which in days of old roused the Roman populace to a delirious pitch of excitement.

How the animal plays were secured makes a thrilling story by itself. Under the direction of the Selig producers, the Selig menagerie was taken to Florida with the stock company last winter and the pictures made there in the open jungle. One of these plays on which patient days were spent is called "Lost in the Jungle."

In keeping with the progress shown in his work with animals, Mr. Selig has sent men to seek material in the tropics and in the far north. The land of the Eskimo has been invaded by Selig camera men, and now real Eskimo dramas, played by real Eskimos in native ice wastes, can be seen. "The Way of the Eskimo," released July 17, is one of them. A valuable polar bear is slain in one of these far north plays and an Eskimo is seen killing the wary walrus by his primitive methods.

A drama now in making shows the pursuit of a bear by a single Indian who is armed only with a knife.

The bear takes to the water and the Indian jumps in after him. The scene, which appears to be laid at the foot of a dashing waterfall in the depth of the forest, was really set in the pool outside the studio, and artificial enough to an onlooker who was present at the rehearsal, proved to be marvelously realistic on the film. The action was both difficult and dangerous, demanding the most patient and arduous rehearsing with the bear, and great bravery on the part of the actor who leaped into the tank with him. After putting the bear through his paces again and again, the beast growing each time more sullen, a dress rehearsal was called with the actor participating. Doubtless the actor's heart beat high before making that first leap into the water, for there was danger of the bear turning upon him. As the bear was swimming directly toward the camera man there was danger for him, too. But all did their parts staunchly, even the bear, and the first effort went off fairly well. After more coaching and prompting and finishing touches the scene was tried again, and this time proved satisfactory. All the "innocent spectators," of whom there were several, began to breathe easy again, feeling that the feat had been finally achieved. But not so, for it is a rule at the Selig plant to take all "big" scenes three times, thereby insuring against possible defect and also giving a choice of action. The Selig standard of perfection demands this. So the whole difficult performance was repeated twice again. Happily the bear, though manifestly unwilling and a trifle peevish, kept his temper to the end and refrained from snapping his collaborator in the pool, or grabbing somebody in a too eager embrace. The thought had been in everybody's mind, however, that he might. For let it not be supposed that these wild beasts have lost their natural fierceness under the softening influence of captivity. Less than ten days ago one of the Selig bears killed his cagemate and own brother in the stillness of the night. Professional jealousy is said to have been the cause. It is possibly this element of danger in associating with the animals that adds zest to the occupation of Selig actors. Instead of fearing the animal films they seem to enjoy them.

From a good sized building at the rear of the yard comes the whirr and hum of busy machinery. This is Selig's experimental department and machine shop. It is surprising to learn that here is maintained constantly at work a force of expert engineers, draftsmen and mechanics, always devising improvements in apparatus and methods, or inventing labor saving systems. This is one of the unique features of the Diamond S plant, and has proven to be worth many times its cost.

The general offices at 20 East Randolph street are interesting in themselves. Besides the usual business transacted at such places, there is maintained a projecting room where are entertained those exhibitors who are ambitious to see the films before they book them, as well as the Chicago police censors and the exchange men. Not only are Selig films shown here, but by a curiously fraternal arrangement the productions of two of his competitors are also exhibited.

It may be interesting to follow the course of a motion picture subject through the great Selig mill, from its entrance in scenario form by way of the United States mail to its distribution in tin boxes to the theaters of the whole world. Hundreds of scenarios are received, most of which are unavailable for some reason or other, just as is the case with literary contributions to popular magazines. But all of them must be read by the scenario editor and his staff. Those that cannot be used are returned to their writers with explanations of their deficiencies. The few available ones are then sent to the main offices, where they are filed away to await their time of production, their authors being paid at once.

When the time comes for using one of the scripts it is assigned a number, which becomes the number of that film throughout its operations. The producer then makes his notes and devises in his mind the "business" of the various scenes. Then must be considered, in their order, locations, properties, costumes, scenery and casts. Each of these items is taken care of by the head of its department and his assistant, in consultation at all times with the producer.

At last everything is ready for the camera. The cast as been arranged, the scenery built and painted, the special properties and costumes bought and fitted. But before a picture is taken each scene must be rehearsed, not once, but many times, until each actor grasps the spirit of the play perfectly. These rehearsals, too, have the advantage of suggesting to the producer those little changes of business or costume that make for perfection of detail. Finally the perfected scenes are filmed, two, three, even four separate negatives being made of each.

The negatives of all the scenes of a film being completed, the next step is to fit them together, selecting the best negative of each scene. The film negative is then projected under the rigid scrutinizing of Mr. Selig, Mr. Nash and other officials of the plant. Here it is that minute flaws of detail, business or photography are detected, and the offending scenes must be taken over again.

But ultimately there is secured a practically perfect negative. The unused secondary negatives of the various scenes are filed in a fireproof vault, to be available in case of emergency. The service negative is taken to the positive process rooms, where many prints are taken from it on rapid automatic printing machines tended by deft-fingered girls, all working by the dim light of ruby lanterns. We have neglected to mention how the raw film stock is obtained from the Eastman Kodak Company at Rochester, N.Y., how it is perforated by special little die punches working in the dark, and comes out ready for the camera and printing machine. Suffice it to say that the finished prints, after inspection, are boxed ready to deliver to the waiting film exchanges—who, in turn, rent them to the theaters, where they are shown to literally millions of delighted pleasure seekers.

It must not be forgotten that the Selig Pacific coast branch, situated at Edendale, Cal., is almost as large as the home plant itself. Beautiful grounds and buildings covering several acres are devoted to the taking, developing and printing of films. Two stock companies and two producers are in active operation here all the time. It is an entirely independent organization under the management of Francis Boggs, who acknowledges no master by Mr. Selig himself. Between the two plants an average of five reels per week is produced. Aside from the land directly owned and occupied by the western organization, there are many localities over which Selig owns the exclusive right to take pictures. Practically all the old picturesque Spanish missions in California are so leased by Selig. One will look in vain for them in other films. The fire department of Los Angeles has granted Selig a similar exclusive concession. Part of the western stock company is generally traveling, seeking out picturesque backgrounds for drama. Mr. Bosworth's recent excursion to Yosemite valley with a company of players under his command has been productive of several films of exceptional pictorial merit.

Edendale, where the Selig California plant is located is a very beautiful suburb of Los Angeles. It is the motion picture center of the Pacific Coast, for there are several other studios there besides Selig's. With clear air and sunshine three hundred days out of the year, conditions are ideal for perfect picture making. The scenic advantages of the location, too, are unique. From "Selig Heights"—an extensive piece of property leased by the year for the Diamond S—can be seen the Pacific Ocean, twenty-two miles to the west, and the broad panorama of Southern California, with its fruit and stock ranches, its snowcapped mountains and its tropical vegetation, to the east, north and south. Within a short distance of Edendale may be found every known variety of national scenery, seemingly arranged by a master producer expressly for the motion picture camera. Within the limits of Selig Heights itself are all the woods, valleys, lakes, rivers, and ruined edifices that could be used in an ordinary picture.

In this enchanted land Director Boggs spends his time devising and producing those startling and spectacular Selig westerns which have excited so much comment. Just now, for example, he has taken his company to the Santa Cruz Islands, where they will camp and "rough it" for a time. They are equipped with a remarkable fleet of boats of all kinds, from a little motor boat to a two masted schooner, and we may look for some interesting marine pictures in the course of time. This kind of work may be called Mr. Bogg's specialty. Of an artistic rather than a commercial temperament, he devotes most of his time to the production end, although he enjoys the title of general manager of the western plant. The business details fall upon the capable shoulders of James L. McGee, assistant business manager.

The studio of the Edendale plant is not so large as the Chicago studio, because of the opportunities for outdoor work. The plant has, however, very complete business offices, property rooms, dressing rooms, etc., as well as a negative developing plant. The negatives, after local inspection and perfection, are sent to Chicago for printing. In the big property rooms may be found every possible requirement, from a toothpick to "Old Hickory," the U.S. mail coach, for which Mr. Selig paid some $2,000, bidding against Buffalo Bill and some of his own competitors. For all excursions automobiles are used, and the plant has a completely equipped large garage.

To this veritable western fairyland W. N. Selig goes in person two or three times a year; and his coming is always regarded as a gala day, for he is a good friend to all his employes from the meanest to the highest. Frequently on such occasions, all work is stopped for the nonce, while "the governor" and his staff pass the balance of the day in the festivities of some dining hall or baseball park.

The rise of the Selig Polyscope Company is one of the marvels of modern business. The wonder of it may be indicated by the expansion of its quarters. From a single room in a small building on an obscure Chicago side street, the business has branched out until now, fifteen years later, it occupies two large manufactories with extensive branch offices in New York and London. The original investment of a few hundred dollars now measures in the hundred thousands, and probably a million dollars or more would not be an excessive estimate to put on the value of the Selig properties.

The little establishment at 43 Peck court, Chicago, started in 1896, was in very truth a humble beginning. It was the factory and salesroom of the Selig Multoscope Company, also the home of W. N. Selig. Those were the days of great hope, arduous endeavor, and strict economy. Over the trials and hardships of those early days memory has kindly drawn a curtain; suffice it to say, that Mr. Selig is a self-made man. For a time Mr. Selig manufactured slides, and his efforts must have been attended with success, for shortly we find the business occupying two floors of the little Peck court building, and the firm name changed to Selig Polyscope Company. The subtle shade of difference between "multo" and "poly" indicates the extent of this modest but substantial development. Later Mr. Selig began to manufacture films, principally "fire scenes" and other subjects caught in the open—no dramas. That was in the days of the open market, when, having made a film, you simply went out and sold it to whosoever would buy. Then, in 1898, which may be called the Selig annus mirabilis, there came to Mr. Selig one Tom Nash, an erstwhile electrician, but who joined the Selig forces as a moving picture operator. Tom Nash was one of the biggest "finds" of Mr. Selig's career, and has followed the Selig destinies ever since, now serving as general superintendent of the big Chicago plant.

In the seven years between 1900 and 1907 the Selig Polyscope Company advanced with leaps and bounds. It was in the latter year that the Chicago plant was opened. A little later the Pacific coast branch was established, first simply as a traveling company, but now with permanent quarters that rival the home plant itself. The Edendale plant employs about 100 people; the Chicago plant something over 200. The substantiality and efficient equipment of these two plants prove that the Selig Polyscope Company is building for the future, proclaiming louder than any words a firm faith in the permanence of the business.

When one says the "Selig Polyscope Company" one really means W. N. Selig himself, who is the presiding genius and leading spirit of the establishment. His eye is on every detail of the business at all times. He is always "there." From eight o'clock in the morning to 5:30 at night, Mr. Selig labors harder than any of his assistants. Like most "big" men, Mr. Selig is democratic and unassuming, talking little of the Selig achievements further than to give his employes all the credit. And just as positively the employes disavow all credit to themselves, heaping it at the feet of Selig. One finds no "big I's" at the Selig plant, but rather a mutual admiration society. The loyalty of Mr. Selig's associates and subordinates throws a flattering light on his character as a man and employer.

A few blocks to the south of the Selig plant lies Riverview Park, the Coney Island of Chicago. You glimpse the top of its gay towers as you leave the Selig door. But Riverview has few allurements now. After tasting the sensations of the Selig plant what has Riverview to offer? Its thrills are now like stale champagne.

As you leave this fascinating domain of motion-picturedom, whose monarch is Selig, you feel a stirring of wonder as you try to comprehend the meaning of the place. All this great aggregation of brains, brawn and matter, for the sake of what? Illusion. The illusion of life known as dramatic art. The Selig plant is an enormous art factory, where film plays are turned out with the same amount of organized efficiency, division of labor and manipulation of matter as if they were locomotives or sewing machines. When you leave the Selig plant you respect the motion picture as you never did before. If in some idle moment you have charged the film play with cheapness, flimsiness and impermanence, you penitently turn about on the Selig threshold and take it all back.

His Father's Bugle. *Louise Kelly. January 27, 1912.*

When Women Rule. *Harry Lonsdale, Myrtle Stedman.*
February 26, 1912.

As Told by Princess Bess. *Princess Redwing. March 1, 1912.*

The Brotherhood of Man. *Kathlyn Williams, Myrtle Stedman. March 7, 1912.*

The Slip. *Winifred Greenwood, Rex de Roselli. March 14, 1912.*

Sons of the Northwoods. *Charles Clary. March 25, 1912.*

All on Account of Checkers. *The Selig Comedy Company. March 29, 1912.*

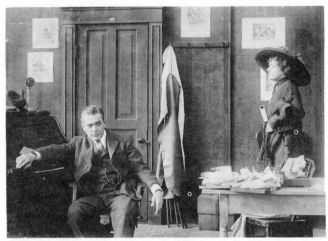

The Other Woman. *Charles Clary, Myrtle Stedman. April 15, 1912.*

Driftwood. *Kathlyn Williams. April 9, 1912.*

A Citizen in the Making. *Winifred Greenwood, William Duncan. April 20, 1912.*

Bessie's Dream. *Bessie Eyton. April 19, 1912. ½ reel.*

The Law of the North. *Adrienne Kroell, Charles Clary.*
April 23, 1912.

Exposed by the Dictograph. *Myrtle Stedman. April*
29, 1912.

The Katzenjammer Kids. *Lillian Brown Leighton,*
John Lancaster. May 3, 1912.

The Coming of Columbus. *May 6, 1912. 3¼ reels.*
Pope Pius X gave Selig a medal for this production.

According to Law. *May 12, 1912.*

The Love of an Island Maid. *Bessie Eyton, Tom Santschi, Hobart Bosworth. May 13, 1912.*

The Girl with the Lantern. *Kathlyn Williams. May 23, 1912.*

Land Sharks vs. Sea Dogs. *Frank Clark, Hobart Bosworth. May 23, 1912.*

The Last Dance. *Charles Clary, Kathlyn Williams.*
June 4, 1912.

Mistaken Identity. *Anna Dodge, Myrtle Stedman.*
June 7, 1912. ½ reel.

The Vision Beautiful. *Tom Santschi, Herbert Rawlin-son. June 13, 1912.*

The Adopted Son. *Kathlyn Williams, Charles Clary. June 24, 1912.*

Murray, the Masher. *Adrienne Kroell, Winifred Green-wood. June 28, 1912.*

The Lake of Dreams. *Tom Santschi. July 1, 1912.*

The Cat and the Canary. *Mr. & Mrs. Frank Weed. July 2, 1912.*

Under Suspicion. *Adrienne Kroell and Winifred Greenwood. July 8, 1912.*

The Vow of Ysobel. *Al E. Garcia, Betty Harte, Herbert Rawlinson. July 9, 1912.*

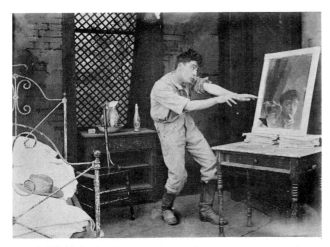

A Mail Order Hypnotist. *July 12, 1912. ½ reel.*

The Pennant Puzzle. *John Lancaster. July 15, 1912.*

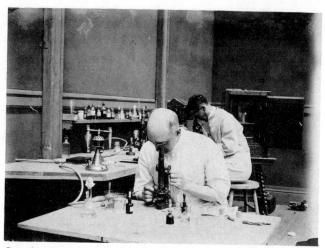

On the Trail of the Germs. *A semi-documentary edu-cational subject. July 22, 1912.*

The Miller of Burgandy. *Hobart Bosworth. July 24, 1912.*

Officer Murray. *Charles Clary. August 1, 1912.*

The Girl at the Cupola. *Charles Clary. August 8, 1912.*

A Messenger to Kearney. *Hobart Bosworth. August 12,*
1912.

In the Tents of the Agra. *Bessie Eyton and Hobart Bosworth. August 15, 1912.*

The Box Car Baby. *August 19, 1912.*

Betty Fools Dear Old Dad. *Goldie Colwell. August 22, 1912.*

Sergeant Byrne of the N.W.M.P. *Eugenie Besserer, Tom Santschi, Wheeler Oakman. September 5, 1912.*

The Indelible Stain. *Bessie Eyton, Tom Santschi, Wheeler Oakman. September 12, 1912.*

The Trade Gun Bullet. *Elaine Davis, Hobart Bosworth, Wheeler Oakman, Herbert Rawlinson. September 13, 1912*

The Pity of It. *Tom Santschi. September 26, 1912.*

How the Cause Was Won. *Betty Harte, Wheeler Oakman. October 2, 1912.*

The Pirate's Daughter. *Betty Harte. October 2, 1912.*

The Great Drought. *Bessie Eyton, Tom Santschi, Al E. Garcia. October 3, 1912.*

Euchred. *George Hernandez, Bessie Eyton, Tom Santschi. October 10, 1912.*

My Wife's Bonnet. *Rose Evans, Lillian Brown Leighton, Frances Baylace. October 14, 1912.*

The Count of Monte Cristo. *Released in 3 reels October 14, 1912. Dantes is entrusted with a letter by the dying captain. Robert Chandler, Hobart Bosworth.*

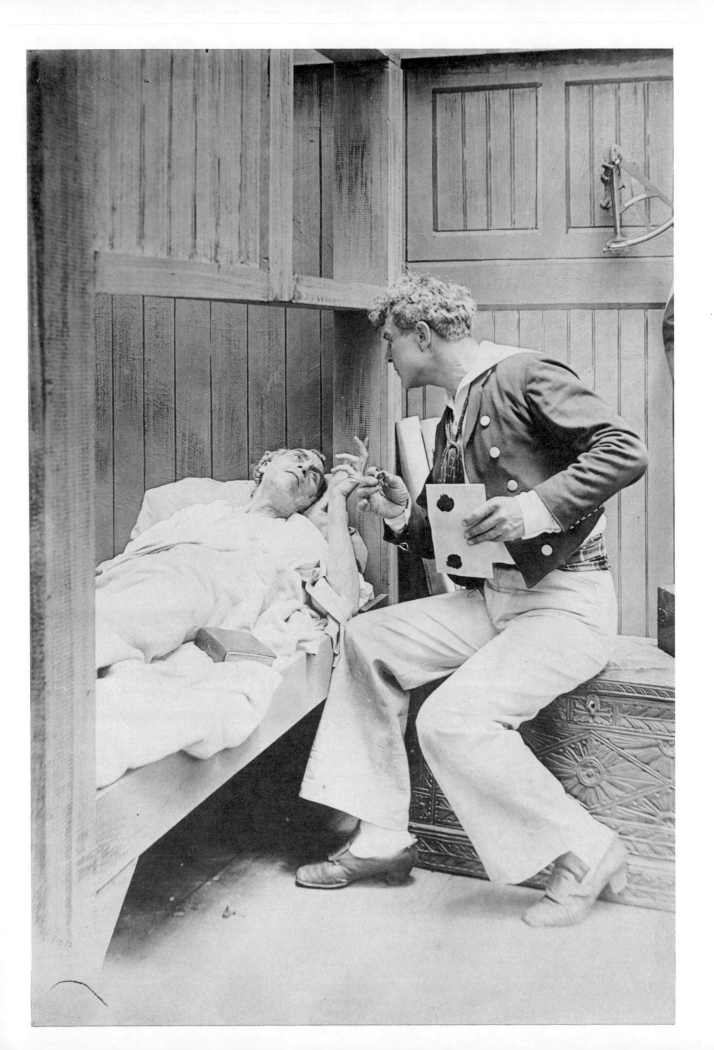

The Count of Monte Cristo. *Morrell is well pleased
with Dantes' work. Hobart Bosworth, Nick Cogley,
George Hernandez and William Hutchinson.*

The Count of Monte Cristo. *Villefort and Fernand
plot the death of Dantes. Roy Watson, Frank Clark.*

The Count of Monte Cristo. *During a prenuptial party at the Reserve Inn, Dantes is charged with conspiracy. William Hutchinson, Hobart Bosworth, Nick Cogley, Eugenie Besserer.*

The Count of Monte Cristo. *Dantes trades places with the dead Abbe and is cast into the sea to freedom.*

The Count of Monte Cristo. *The Abbe Faria (Fred Huntly) provides Dantes with a means of escape.*

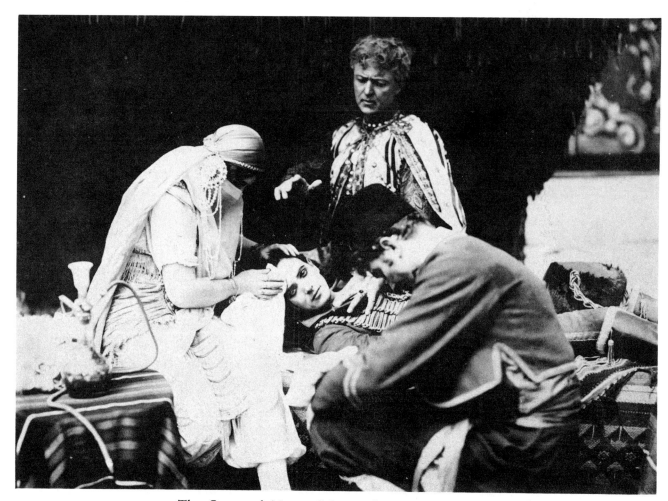

The Count of Monte Cristo. *Claiming the Abbe's hidden treasure, Dantes lives with Arabs and saves the life of a French Army captain, who later turns out to be his son. Here Haidee (Bessie Eyton) nurses the wounded man to health.*

The Count of Monte Cristo. *Reproduction of part of an advertisement for the film.*

The Shuttle of Fate. *Tom Santschi. October 16, 1912.*

The Fisherboy's Faith. *Tom Santschi, Bessie Eyton,
Anna Dodge. October 28, 1912.*

Carmen of the Isles. *Herbert Rawlinson, Bessie Eyton.*
November 7, 1912.

The Legend of the Lost Arrow. *Hobart Bosworth,*
Bessie Eyton, Herbert Rawlinson. November 8, 1912.

Saved by a Fire. *November 11, 1912.*

Shanghaied. *Bessie Eyton, Anna Dodge, Herbert Rawlinson. November 15, 1912.*

Atala. *Hobart Bosworth. November 20, 1912.*

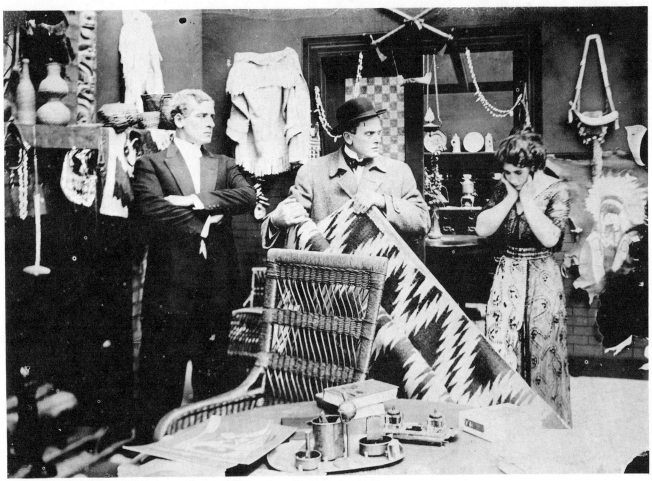

The Triangle. *Tom Santschi, Herbert Rawlinson, Bessie Eyton. November 28, 1912.*

John Colter's Escape. *Bessie Eyton (in pigtails), Herbert Rawlinson (lead runner). December 6, 1912.*

The Vintage of Fate. *Eugenie Besserer. December 9, 1912.*

Opitsah *(Apache for Sweetheart). Tom Santschi, Bessie Eyton. December 16, 1912.*

The Millionaire Vagabonds. *Wheeler Oakman. December 18, 1912.*

Our Lady of Pearls. *Herbert Rawlinson, Goldie Colwell. December 30, 1912.*

8

The Coming of Columbus[1]

The Selig Polyscope Company at last offers to the world the great historical spectacle of the discovery of America. This result of many months of conscientious labor is a credit to motography and a great contribution to the cause of education.

REVIEWED BY JAMES S. McQUADE

I recollect that, in his essay on "The Decline and Fall of the Roman Empire," Macaulay compared the author, in his undertaking of the gigàntic task, to a lone axeman chopping his way through a primeval forest of unknown extent and difficulties. And, somehow, in beginning this review of "The Coming of Columbus," I am impressed that when William N. Selig first dreamt of filming this tremendous subject he must have felt somewhat like Macaulay's lone axeman, because of the bewildering barriers in his path. The great historian Gibbons struggled amid the abundance of myths and legends from which he had to sift the wheat of historical data; the filmer of "The Coming of Columbus" was puzzled what course to pursue, because of the great wealth of historical data right at hand. The difficulty lay in selecting the incidents that would best serve to portray the life and character of the Great Discoverer in a worthy manner, and on a scale that would fully measure up to the heights of his renown.

There is a halo around Columbus that is clearly seen by the great eye of civilized humanity, and his lifework will inspire the human race as long as it will endure; and I am strong in the belief that his life, as revealed in the Selig pictures, is the greatest achievement yet wrought by cinematography. "The Coming of Columbus" is destined to win millions of new patrons for the moving picture; for the interest in it will be world wide, and it will clearly demonstrate the value and serviceability of the moving picture in the narration of notable historical and epochal themes.

To have undertaken the production of these films without careful research, well laid plans, the necessary facilities and abundant resources, would have resulted in regrettable failure. And, in addition to all these, the exact counterparts of the three caravels—the Santa Maria, the Pinta and the Nina—were required to give due realism to the story. Mr. Selig was especially fortunate in this respect; for, anchored in Yacht cove, in Jackson Park, the three vessels referred to have been in the care of the South Park Commissioners since the World's Columbian Exposition, in 1893. As is known, the Santa Maria was built in Spain and presented to the Exposition by the Queen Regent, Chris-

1. From: *The Moving Picture World,* September, 1912, pp. 407–10.

124

tina of Spain, being an exact reproduction of the flagship of Columbus. The Pinta and the Nina were reproduced in Spain, according to the most reliable records, by W. McCarty Little, of the United States Navy. These vessels crossed the Atlantic under their own sails, following as closely as possible the original course taken by Columbus. After reaching these shores the caravels were brought north, and passed up the St. Lawrence, through the Welland Canal, across Lakes Erie, Huron and Michigan, and into Chicago harbor.

These invaluable vessels were secured by Mr. Selig for use in the production, a bond of $100,000 being given for their safe return. The Knights of Columbus cooperated earnestly to secure the caravels from the Park Commissioners, the negotiations taking nearly three years before arrangements were made.

In this connection it may be stated that Mr. Selig's forces spent several weeks in docking the caravels and making them seaworthy. Their seams were recaulked, the bottoms painted and the upper works thoroughly overhauled. The rudder of one of the vessels was replaced and new sails were made for all three, at a heavy outlay. The manning of the caravels was another difficult task, as over 120 deep sea water sailors were required to handle them. When the men were secured, it took several weeks to familiarize them with the old style sails, so as to maneuver the vessels as required by the camera man.

It is worthy of note that Mr. Selig succeeded in securing the original log book of Columbus as a property for the Santa Maria. This was done through the kind offices of the Spanish Consul in Chicago, a bond of $10,000 being given for its return. Although this log book in the Santa Maria's cabin will catch but few eyes, its being there is an evidence of the great care taken in the matter of details.

The scenario was written by C. E. Nixon, a well known newspaper man, author, critic and playwright. Mr. Nixon spent three years in study and research for his material, and his completed work was afterwards carefully reviewed by the producing staff of the Selig Polyscope Company. The account left by Columbus of his voyages, and those of his associates, have been faithfully followed in the Selig production. Some of the incidents have been found in official documents and in the Spanish archives, and others have been taken from testimony given in the law suit brought against the Crown of Spain by Diego, the son of Columbus, after the death of his father. The aim throughout has been to give a moving, living picture of Columbus as he was and to keep close to historical accuracy and the atmosphere of the times.

Mr. Selig states that $50,000 has been expended on the three films in "The Coming of Columbus." Over 350 acting people were engaged in the production in addition to a host of supernumeraries and skilled workmen.

"The Coming of Columbus" will be released May 6, by special arrangement with, and under the exclusive control of the General Film Company. Harry J. Cohen, of the Selig Polyscope Co., left Chicago on a flying tour of the country, April 18, in the interest of these films. He will visit all the branch offices of the General Film Co., and private exhibitions will be given licensed exhibitors in the leading cities. Mr. Cohen left for the East and will next visit the South and far West and then the Middle West. His campaign will last 20 days, during which time he will never sleep in a hotel.

The publicity department of the Selig Polyscope has completed arrangements for an extensive advertising campaign for "The Coming of Columbus." Exhibitors can be furnished with all varieties of aids to boom the films by applying to the Chicago office. A special Columbus circular will be mailed them giving all particulars as to prices, etc., of the various aids. A special musical program for the presentation of the films is being prepared for Mr. Selig by S. L. Rothapfel, the widely known manager of the Lyceum theatre, Minneapolis.

The Pictured Story

As is known, Columbus visited nearly every Court in Europe for assistance to carry out his great project. The Selig films introduce him to use in Portugal, where he sought the favor of John II. We see him visit a quaint votive shrine in Portugal accompanied by his son Diego, who is seen leading the lone donkey, which carried their scanty effects. They are on the way to Spain, where the mariner hopes to gain an audience with the good Queen Isabella.

We next see the little party at an old mission in Spain, where Columbus stops and explains his plans and theories to the pious fathers. Most of the latter, we can see, are astounded at his views of geography and shake their heads gravely as they ponder. However,

The captains of the Nina and Pinta attempt to persuade Columbus (Charles Clary) to turn back.

clesiastics, a vestal choir, famous dignitaries and other members of the laity as they march past the royal stand. This is one of the most imposing scenes in the three films and forms a fitting close to the first reel.

And now the three caravels pass before us in order; first the flagship Santa Maria, next the Pinta and then the Nina. They are first seen anchored in the quiet harbor of Palos, from which they set sail on an epoch-making voyage. We catch a glimpse of Sunday mass on board the Santa Maria as the little vessels plow their ways further into the unknown seas. And soon, we notice discontent and disaffection among the sailors. The captains of the smaller craft see it and, half in accord with the spirit, try to influence Columbus to turn back to Spain. They visit him again as mutiny flaunts its face, and we see the intrepid Commander quelling the turbulent spirits by his presence and cheering words of hope.

he interests Fra Antonio, one of the Queen's confessors, who succeeds in getting him an audience with her Majesty. The meeting takes place in the royal tent on the field of Granada, where at the time, a conflict rages between the royal troops and the Moors. Just as Columbus has won the Queen's ear and he has spread his charts on the table, messengers arrive from the battlefield and announce the surrender of the Moors, putting an end to the interview.

Isabella turns Columbus over to the wise men of Salamanca to test his sanity, and one can easily see that they look on him as a mad theorist. But Fra Antonio persuades the Queen to grant Columbus another audience, and we are treated to a splendid Court scene, where Isabella and Ferdinand listen to the great mariner. The Queen offers to sell her jewels to support Columbus on his quest, but she is spared the sacrifice by the generosity of Fernandez, the Court physician, who finances the undertaking. Next we see Columbus made an admiral by King Ferdinand, in presence of the Court, and a great procession of ec-

"Land Ho!"

Shortly afterwards we see the faces of Columbus and others raised aloft in ecstasy, as the lookout cries, "Land Ho!" "Away to the West," he further cries in answer to the Admiral. And then, with hearts full of thankfulness to the Giver of all Good, we see the worn out sailors join with their Commander in offering thanksgiving. Then a bird is caught in the rigging by a sailor, and every eye is strained to catch a glimpse of the shore from which it has flown. Next we view the fleet at anchor and the landing on the island, on the coast of which a body of natives watches the strange white men from the clouds. The standard of Spain is reared on the new soil on which Columbus has first planted the emblem of the cross.

The third reel opens with a magnificent scene showing the welcome extended Columbus and his men at the Court of Ferdinand and Isabella. It is one fully befitting the occasion, and fairly flashes with royal and courtly splendor. In the midst of the great assemblage, where even stoical grandees applaud the success of Columbus, he is knighted by King Ferdinand.

A fine interior scene is devoted to the "egg" incident. We see the insulting courtier, who had tried to belittle the feat of Columbus, humbled by the simple problem of standing an egg on end. This scene is artistically posed and is worthy of being ranked with a great painting. The third voyage is undertaken by Columbus and we see him mourning over the destruction of his colony, La Navidad. Insolent and avaricious Spanish nobles had wrought the ruin, and already they had planned the ruin of the Great Discoverer. While he is endeavoring to rebuild the colony and the fortunes of the natives who love him, Francisco de Boabdilla arrives to take him back in chains to Spain. As the arrest is being made the following proclamation is read:

"Whereas, one Christopher Columbus, governor of the Antilles, has been found guilty of malfeasance in office and has not accounted for much gold promised the Crown—the Commissioner of the Crown, Boabdilla, will cause his arrest and conduct him to Spain for trial.   "FERDINAND."

We see the natives determined to set Columbus free; but we also see him dissuading them from their purpose. Then our blood boils as we watch them riveting the cruel chains on his ankles, and witness the further shame of Spain as he sails away, bound and alone, in the vessel's hold.

The final sub-title in the third reel, "Sic transit gloria virum," is scarcely fitting in this case. True, the honors heaped on a man by the world may pass away, but the glory of great deeds performed by him for the human race cannot pass away. The glory of Columbus is greater now than ever before. While cheated of his right to have the great continent, discovered by him, named after him, the story of his life is known to all, while one is obliged to refer to an encyclopedia for information about Amerigo.

9

Maintaining a Wild Animal Jungle for Pictures[1]

THE DIAMOND-S FARM

A green tract of far-stretching acres in which animals—wild animals—will have the right of way, is the latest dream of W. N. Selig, which has come to pass. The permanent home of the jungle beasts is already being made ready. The accompaniment will be the jingle of more than one hundred thousand dollars. The location is the vicinity of Los Angeles, Cal., which will add to the name and fame of the wonder city.

With him in the venture of forming the world's greatest collection of wild animals, Mr. Selig has chosen Otto Breitkreitz, famed as probably the world's greatest animal trainer and breeder. "Big Otto," he is called, and "Big Otto," he is known to all showmen. He is king in his particular line of work. He is big in stature, weighing three hundred and fifty pounds, and is big in heart and policy. He formerly owned and conducted shows in which wild animals were the chief attraction, and has to his credit the training and breeding of the animals used in the majority of American shows. He has retired from the show business, however, and devotes himself to just the rearing and training of animals which, to him, are pets, but to outsiders, are just brutes.

For years "Big Otto" has been in charge of the

Selig wild animals. He is the genius of the farm where they are at present, in the city of Los Angeles. Here the big trainer, his family, his employees and their families, have their homes. They are pretty little cottages with wide verandas on which baby lions and tiny leopards play. Lion kittens which, having been deserted by their own mother, were adopted by a dog and thus fondly cared for, have been the pets at Foreman Sanders' cottage for the last several weeks. They consider themselves in duty bound to keep at the heels of Mrs. Sanders and when that busy housewife thoughtlessly goes beyond their range, she is reprimanded for her violation of the cub speed law, by a heart-rendering series of meows, for all the world like those of protesting kittens. A baby leopard, beautiful in the markings of its velvety coat, is the cage companion of the cubs.

The jungle wilds of all the world have furnished the specimens of which the Selig farm already boasts and which, in its present consignment, is the biggest and most complete of any individual picture company; and the same jungle wilds will be visited for future additions to the without-the-city-limits tract, to be sacred to bears, tigers, elephants, pumas, camels, hyenas, horses, mules, monkeys, ponies, wolves, dogs, wild goats, jaguars, sacred cattle, raccoons, guinea-pigs, ant-eaters, parrots, geese, ducks and various hybrids.

---

1. From *Motography,* Vol. VIII, No. 10, November 9, 1912, pp. 347–49.

A recent photograph-day at the animal farm put most of the animals on their good behaviour. "Kitty," the puma, however, wasn't inclined to be good even with the incentive of company present. Olga, the adopted daughter of "Big Otto," and who is professionally known as the Princess Cecelia, entered the cage wherein the puma was housed and was forcibly greeted by the occupant, which sprung at her and, before two attendants could come to the rescue, had torn her tailored suit almost to pieces. Three times the puma renewed the attack on the girl and each time the force of her whip drove him back. When help came, she had driven the animal into an adjoining compartment of the cage.

The remainder of the farm specimens, though, were quite agreeable to the suggestion of being photographed. The dog-wolf stood erect and looked into the face of the camera; lion cubs, eight months old, stood side by side and calmly awaited the momentous click; the fierce laughing hyena pointed its ears and showed all its teeth; the sacred ox nibbled amiably at a proffered delicacy; the jaguars rolled over and stretched themselves and one allowed Miss Olga to recline against him and fondle his ears; Duke, the great African lion, selected a pose which showed to best advantage, his massive head and mane, and Toddles responded to Miss Olga's voice and obediently stood with uplifted fore-leg and trunk until the photographer had finished. Toddles is a big fellow,

despite his name, and is a faithful actor in whatever part he is cast. His meagre requirement is two bales of hay, daily. Toddles was the star performer in the film, "Lost in the Jungle," in which, during his wanderings through the forest, he found the heroine lying exhausted on the ground and, kneeling, he lifted her to his back and thus bore her to safety. While not acting he stands patiently day after day, chained to a tree, appreciative of meal times, and the fragmentary conversation of the keepers.

The lion, Duke, who weighs six hundred and fifty pounds, is said to be the largest in captivity, and is a splendid beast. He is the father of several dozen cubs which vary in age from four weeks to eight months. Many of the animals answer when called by name.

The proposition of the keep of the farm's wild inhabitants is a big one. For the carnivorous ones, two horses are slaughtered daily as the meat has been found to be preferable to beef. For the young or sick creatures, ducks, geese and rabbits are raised as food.

The animals are divided into groups, there being five trainers and each trainer has his own particular set of animals which obey him implicitly.

The enlarged animal farm, soon to become a reality, was sought for by San Diego. But the house of Selig is partial to Los Angeles on account of its large plant already near there; so the Los Angeles neighborhood it is to be.

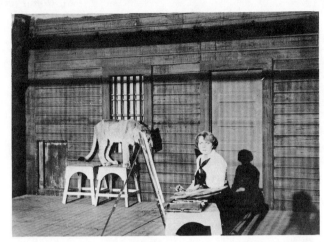

The Artist and the Brute. *Kathlyn Williams. February 7, 1913.*

A Black Hand Elopement. *Lillian Hayward. January 22, 1913.*

A Plain Girl's Love. *Bessie Eyton, Tom Santschi. January 15, 1913.*

The Miner's Justice. *Frank Clark. January 27, 1913.*

The Lesson. *Lillian Hayward, Master Timmy Sheehan,
Charles Clary. January 30, 1913.*

The Altar of the Aztecs. *Hobart Bosworth, Phyllis Gordon. January 31, 1913.*

Sweeney and the Million. *George Cox, Lillian Brown Leighton, John Lancaster. February 4, 1913.*

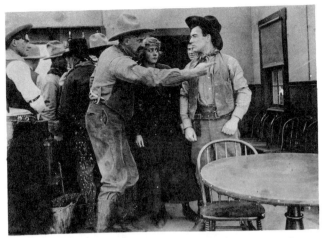

How it Happened. *Lester Cuneo, Myrtle Stedman, William Duncan. February 6, 1913. That's Tom Mix at the far left.*

Pierre of the North. *Dorothy Davenport, Hobart Bosworth, Al E. Garcia. February 10, 1913.*

Bill's Birthday Present. *Lester Cuneo, William Duncan. February 13, 1913.*

A Little Hero. *Roy Clark, Baby Lillian Wade. February 14, 1913. ½ reel.*

Two Men and a Woman. *Henry W. Otto, Harold Lockwood, Kathlyn Williams. February 17, 1913.*

The Early Bird. *Tom Santschi. February 19, 1913.*

Nobody's Boy. *Adrienne Kroell. February 20, 1913.*

Yankee Doodle Dixie. *Eleanor Blevins, William Hutchinson. February 26, 1913.*

The Bank's Messenger. *Myrtle Stedman, William Duncan. February 27, 1913.*

The Story of Lavinia. *March 5, 1913.*

The Spanish Parrot-Girl. *Harold Lockwood, Henry W. Otto. March 6, 1913.*

Love before Ten. *Baby Lillian Wade, Roy Clark, Henry W. Otto. March 17, 1913.*

Turn Him Out. *Thomas Flynn, Lillian Brown Leighton. March 18, 1913.*

The Old Clerk. *Eddie James, Herbert Rawlinson, Anna Dodge, William Hutchinson. March 24, 1913.*

Sally in our Alley. *Wheeler Oakman, Bessie Eyton.*
March 28, 1913.

The Prisoner of Cabanas. *Bessie Eyton. March 31,*
1913.

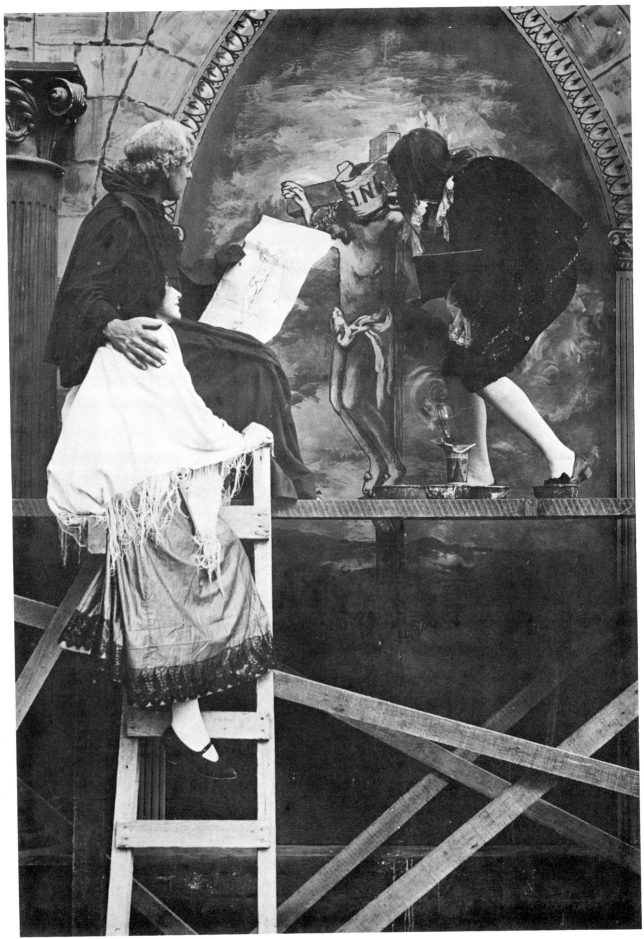

Vengeance Is Mine. *Bessie Eyton, Tom Santschi,*
Wheeler Oakman. April 7, 1913.

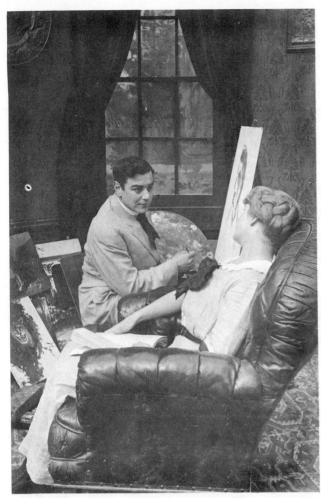

With Love's Eyes. *Al E. Garcia, Kathlyn Williams. April 11, 1913.*

The Woodsman's Daughter. *Herbert Rawlinson, April 14, 1913.*

Alas! Poor Yorick. *Roscoe Arbuckle, John Lancaster, Frank Clark, Tom Santschi, Lillian Hayward. April 21, 1913.*

The Burglar Who Robbed Death. *Kathlyn Williams,*
Baby Lillian Wade. April 30, 1913.

An Old Actor. *Frank Clark. May 5, 1913.*

Belle Boyd, a Confederate Spy. *Winifred Greenwood (holding flowers). May 7, 1913.*

In the Days of Witchcraft. *Eugenie Besserer, Hobart Bosworth, Herbert Rawlinson. May 9, 1913.*

Lieutenant Jones. *Eugenie Besserer, Al W. Filson, Kathlyn Williams. May 13, 1913.*

In the Long Ago. *Wheeler Oakman, Bessie Eyton. May 15, 1913.*

Buck Richard's Bride. *George Williams, Hobart Bosworth, Margarita Loveridge, Herbert Rawlinson. May 14, 1913.*

The Tattle Battle. *Baby Lillian Wade, Audrey Little-field. May 20, 1913. ½ reel.*

A Flag of Two Wars. *William Scott, Herbert Rawlinson. June 3, 1913.*

When Lillian Was Little Red Riding Hood. *Baby Lillian Wade, Bessie Eyton. June 16, 1913. ½ reel.*

Mrs. Hilton's Jewels. *Kathlyn Williams, Henry W. Otto. June 18, 1913.*

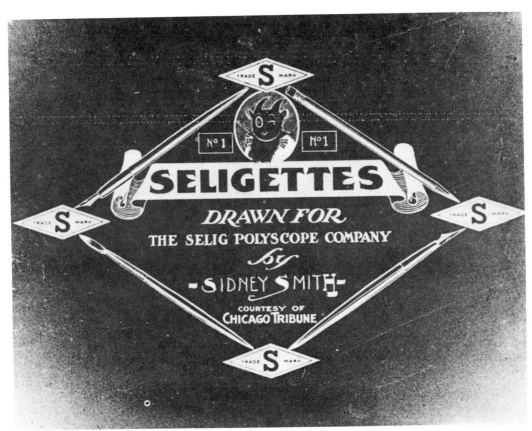

Old Doc Yak. *July 8, 1913. ½ reel.*

A Wild Ride. *Wheeler Oakman. July 12, 1913.*

Touch of a Child. *Henry W. Otto, Mabel Van Buren.*
July 19, 1913.

Child of the Sea. *Herbert Rawlinson, Al W. Filson,*
Kathlyn Williams. August 18, 1913.

The Lonely Heart. *Myrtle Stedman. September 2, 1913.*

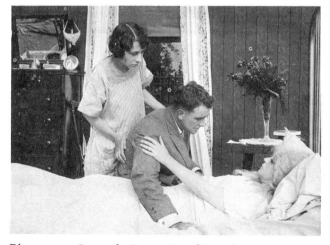

Phantoms. *Gertrude Ryan, Harold Lockwood, Eugenie Besserer. November 10, 1913. 2 reels.*

Whose Wife Is This? *Tom Santschi, Bessie Eyton. November 10, 1913.*

Outwitted by Billy. *Stella Razetto, Guy Oliver. November 21, 1913.*

Mounted Officer Flynn. *Mabel Van Buren, Baby Lillian Wade, Joe King. November 25, 1913.*

Northern Hearts. *Guy Oliver, Stella Razetto, Harold Lockwood. December 5, 1913.*

Master of the Garden. *Wheeler Oakman, Bessie Eyton. December 8, 1913. 2 reels.*

Don't Let Mother Know *or* The Bliss of Ignorance.
Louise Kelly, Adrienne Kroell. December 11, 1913.

The Mysterious Way. *Joe King, Baby Lillian Wade,
Mabel Van Buren. December 12, 1913. 2 reels.*

Until the Sea. *Frank Clark, Bessie Eyton. December 18,*
1913.

Lure of the Road. *Stella Razetto, Guy Oliver. Decem-*
ber 19, 1913.

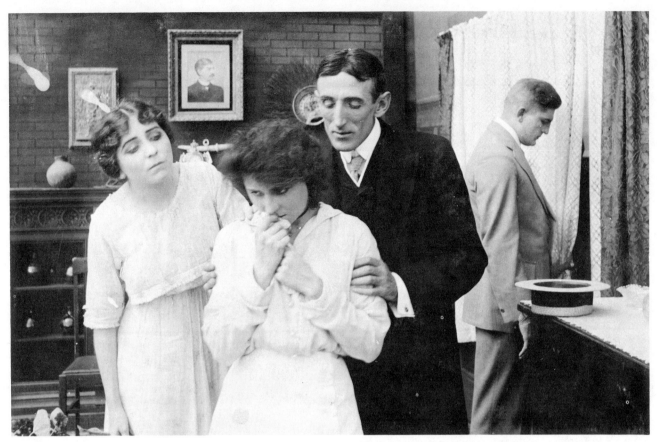

His Sister. *Adda Gleason, Stella Razetto, Jack McDonald, Lamar Johnstone. December 26, 1913.*

The Adventures of Kathlyn. *A 13-episode serial released December 29, 1913 with Chapter 1, "The Unwelcome Throne." Tom Santschi and Kathlyn Williams.*

The Adventures of Kathlyn. *Gilson Willets wrote the story for Miss Williams.*

The Adventures of Kathlyn. *Charles Clary furnished the villainy in this popular chapter play which saw a waltz named after the star.*

The Adventures of Kathlyn. *Charles Clary offers our heroine a sorry choice.*

The Adventures of Kathlyn. *Kathlyn Williams and Goldie Colwell. Three years later, the 27 reels were recut into an 8-reel feature and reissued. Although Miss Williams had made many Selig films, it was this serial that brought her to international fame.*

Buster and Sunshine. *Bessie Eyton. January 2, 1914.*

Unto the Third and Fourth Generation. *Guy Oliver (right). January 5, 1914. 2 reels.*

Blue Blood and Red. *Margaret Loveridge. January 15, 1914.*

Tony and Maloney. *Mabel Van Buren. February 6, 1914. ½ reel.*

The Mistress of His House. *Lillian Hayward, Stella Razetto. February 12, 1914.*

Through the Centuries. *Henry W. Otto, Mabel Van Buren. February 17, 1914.*

Memories. *Guy Oliver, Al W. Filson. February 20, 1914.*

The Attic Above. *Henry W. Otto. February 27, 1914.*

The Tragedy of Ambition *or* Madge O'Mara. *Wheeler Oakman, Bessie Eyton. March 2, 1914. 2 reels.*

The Smuggler's Sister *or* Duty. *Wheeler Oakman.*
March 3, 1914.

Little Lillian Turns the Tide. *Baby Lillian Wade.*
March 5, 1914.

Kid Pink and the Maharajah. *Guy Oliver, Al. W. Filson. March 12, 1914.*

Two Little Vagabonds. *Roy Clark, Max Verner. March 20, 1914.*

The Midnight Call. *Mabel Van Buren. March 31, 1914. ½ reel.*

When Thieves Fall Out. *Harold Lockwood. April 1, 1914.*

The Fire Jugglers. *Guy Oliver, Bessie Eyton. April 9, 1914.*

The Cherry Pickers. *Wheeler Oakman, Bessie Eyton. April 13, 1914. 2 reels.*

Shotgun Jones. *Wheeler Oakman, Joseph Girard, Hoot Gibson, Bessie Eyton. April 27, 1914. 2 reels.*

The Baby Spy. *Baby Lillian Wade. May 25, 1914. 2 reels.*

The Hopeless Dawn. *Bessie Eyton, Gertrude Ryan.*
May 27, 1914.

The Girl behind the Barrier. *Stella Razetto. May 30,*
1914.

When the Night Call Came. *Guy Oliver, Eugenie Besserer. June 13, 1914.*

In Defiance of the Law. *Wheeler Oakman. June 14, 1914.*

Reporter Jimmy Intervenes. *Al W. Filson, Gul Oliver.*
July 6, 1914. 2 reels.

His Fight. *Eugenie Besserer, Wheeler Oakman, Henry*
W. Otto. July 11, 1914.

Footprints. *Al W. Filson, Lillian Hayward, Guy Oliver, George Hernandez. July 25, 1914.*

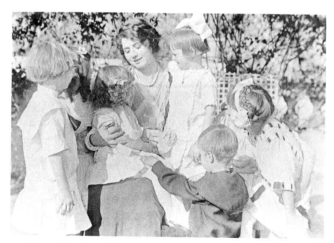

The Mother Heart. *Bessie Eyton, July 29, 1914.*

Etienne of the Glad Heart. *Bessie Eyton, Tom Santschi, Tom Mix. August 3, 1914.*

The Reporter on the Case. *Stella Razetto, Guy Oliver.*
August 5, 1914.

Willie. *Wheeler Oakman. August 10, 1914. 2 reels.*

The Speck on the Wall. *Wheeler Oakman, Kathlyn Williams. August 17, 1914.*

What Became of Jane? *Stella Razetto, Al W. Filson. August 22, 1914.*

Chip of the Flying U. *Frank Clark, Tom Mix. August 29, 1914. 3 reels.*

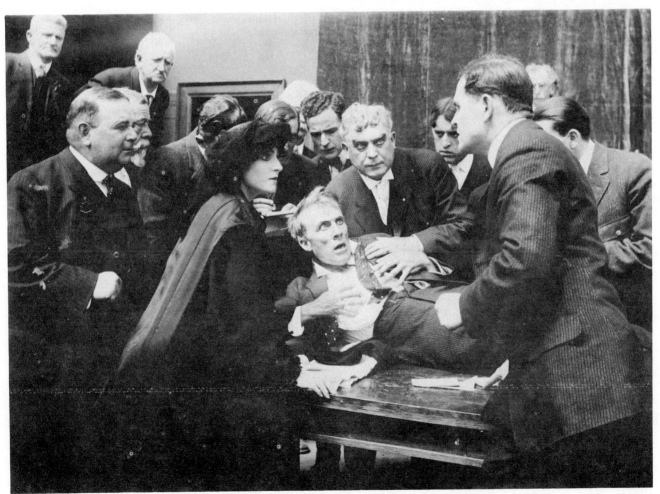

Who Killed George Graves? *George Hernandez, Stella Razetto, Fred Huntly, Al W. Filson, Guy Oliver. August 31, 1914. 2 reels.*

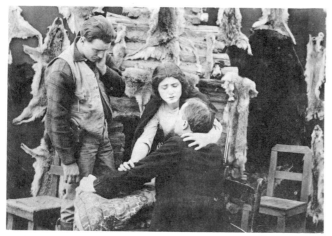

When the West Was Young. *Wheeler Oakman, Bessie Eyton. September 7, 1914.*

A Typographical Error. *Guy Oliver, Fred Huntly,*
Stella Razetto. September 8, 1914.

Ye Vengeful Vagabonds. *September 13, 1914.*

Ye Vengeful Vagabonds. *Guy Oliver, Stella Razetto.*
September 13, 1914.

The Lonesome Trail. *Wheeler Oakman, Gertrude*
Ryan. September 18, 1914.

The Going of the White Swan. *Frank Clark, Tom Mix. September 28, 1914.*

Hearts and Masks. *Wheeler Oakman, Kathlyn Williams. October 1, 1914.*

The Woman of It. *Kathlyn Williams, Charles Clary, Wheeler Oakman. October 17, 1914.*

The Tragedy that Lived. *Wheeler Oakman, Kathlyn Williams, Charles Clary. October 24, 1914.*

The Wasp. *Fred Huntly, Guy Oliver, Stella Razetto. October 28, 1914.*

C. D. *Stella Razetto, Guy Oliver. November 4, 1914.*

The Losing Fight. *Wheeler Oakman, Kathlyn Williams. November 7, 1914.*

Peggy of Primrose Lane. *Guy Hernandez, Stella Razetto. November 11, 1914.*

The Story of the Blood Red Rose. *Kathlyn Williams,
Charles Clary. November 11, 1914.*

Her Sacrifice. *Wheeler Oakman, Kathlyn Williams,
Charles Clary. November 21, 1914.*

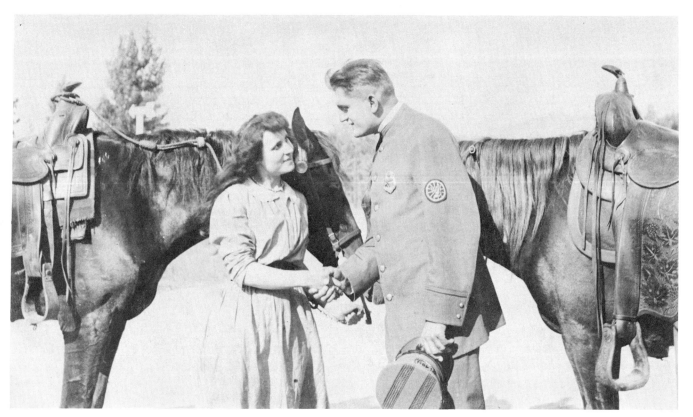

Fate and Ryan. *Stella Razetto, Lamar Johnstone. November 28, 1914.*

One Traveler Returns. *George Hernandez, Mrs. Guy Oliver, Stella Razetto, Lamar Johnstone, Adda Gleason. December 23, 1914.*

10

The Selig Polyscope[1]

EDITOR'S NOTE: *During the approximately two decades of production, the Selig Polyscope was never a popular projector in comparison to the Edison, Powers and Motiograph machines but it proved to be the mainstay of the early Selig operation. Few complete models of the Polyscope are to be found today and little was ever published concerning its use or operation. The accompanying article by David S. Hulfish was published in 1913 and deals in brief with the second and final Polyscope model.*

The old style Polyscope, made by the Selig Company, has been withdrawn from the market. It used the pin-shift mechanism controlled by two cams on the main driving shaft. . . .

The film feeding mechanism is the American standard, three-sprocket, with Geneva intermittent drive.

In threading up the film, the feed reel is placed in the magazine on the top of the motion head, the end of the film is taken through the film outlet rollers, and the door of the feed magazine is closed.

By finger pressure upon a projecting lug, the presser roller is lifted from the upper constant feed sprocket until the film is placed upon the sprocket and meshed with the teeth.

The frame lever is now framed "down" to take out any slack which might be above the film gate, the film is placed in the track of the film gate with a slight slack above—at least one picture length—then meshed with the intermittent sprocket, and the film-gate door is closed. This causes the guide roller at the top of the door to engage the edges of the film, and presses the presser roller against the intermittent sprocket, both of these rollers being carried by the door. This step in threading might seem at first to require three hands on the operator, but the trick is to hold the end of the film below the intermittent with the left hand, to press the film above the motion-head frame with the long finger of the right hand and stretch it tight over the film window and along the film track of the gate, then to swing the door shut with the thumb of the right hand, which will be almost engaging the top guide roller of the gate.

Now frame "up" and give a little slack in the lower feed loop, then pass the film down into the magazine box, or to the take-up reel if one is used.

The Selig lamp house has the feature of sliding the lamp entirely out of the house to make inside adjustments, and to set the carbons . . . the lamp [may be] withdrawn from the lamp house. Before projection is begun, the lamp is pushed in until the vertical panel at the back of the lamp closes with the body of the lamp house and forms a closed house. The controlling knobs have universal joints, permitting them to pass through very small holes in the back panel of the lamp house, and yet reach and operate their different parts of the lamp in any position of adjustment.

Four knobs are provided outside the lamp house, for lateral, transverse, vertical, and feed movements of lamp. The angle of the carbons, either jointly for

1. Extracted from **MOTION PICTURE WORK** by David S. Hulfish, American School of Correspondence, Chicago, 1913, pp. 149–153.

direct current or separately for alternating current, is adjusted by drawing the lamp from the house and working upon adjustments normally inside of the lamp house. . . .

Coming attractions were announced to audiences well into the twenties via glass slides projected on the screen. While many theatres used separate lantern slide projectors for this purpose, some manufacturers like Selig provided an accessory slide carrier for use with their equipment.

The accompanying cut is a facsimile of

THE SELIG POLYSCOPE COMPANY'S

NEW IMPROVED STEEL

Fire-Proof Slide-Carrier

It is the height of perfection and mechanical simplicity; quick in response to the touch and works exceptionally smooth, but not with the annoying looseness common in carriers of former device previously on the market.

This carrier complies with every requirement of Fire Underwriters of all cities.

All stock carefully constructed and tested.

Ready for shipment.   Order now.

Price,   -   -   - $1.50 Each

Selig's fire-proof slide-carrier.

11

"The Spoilers"[1]

*Rex E. Beach's Famous Romance of Alaska Realistically Visualized in
Nine Reels by the Selig Polyscope Co.*

REVIEWED BY JAMES S. McQUADE

The inaugural presentation of "The Spoilers" at
Orchestra Hall, Chicago, on Wednesday, March 25,
was given before a notable audience. About 2000
people took advantage of the invitations sent out by
the Selig Polyscope Company, and they represented
leading men and women in the professions, business
and art and society circles. Some of them, no doubt,
viewed moving pictures for the first time; but the fre-
quent applause that marked the telling incidents
showed that all enjoyed the occasion with an enthusiasm akin to that of a schoolboy.

When one views a moving picture for the first
time, as I did in this case, and is a witness of the
impressions created on the minds of such a distinguished gathering, he cannot help feeling that any
review of his will be inadequate without a due consideration of the intelligent opinions of the many
others. In a word, my opinion at the close of the
presentation was that the story is a great one, and that
it has been filmed in a way that is also great—great
in direction, acting and photography—and that opinion was made still stronger by the clearly expressed
opinions of the many others in the select audience.

I have read the Beach romance several times, and I
must confess that it has always held me in thrall—
not at points, but all the way through. It is a red-

blooded story, saturated through and through with
the spirit of the "Old West"—the West of the forty-
niners, although it treats of the middle nineties. The
old California of the earlier years was recreated at
Dawson and Nome, by reason of the isolation of far
Alaskan points from the national government. Law
in its technical operation was unknown. Men protected their rights by might, either by brawn or gun,
when elemental justice was violated. And everyone
knows that this law of might is exceedingly dangerous,
but much more so when the semblance and not the
spirit of the law is set working.

The Rex Beach story shows that an iniquitous
scheme was plotted and hatched in Washington by
which the semblance of law was placed in power at
Nome; and it shows in most convincing fashion that
men's sense of elemental justice won out against it.
This sense of elemental justice in all of us forces us
heart and soul to espouse the cause of the miners, led
by Glenister, rather than that of McNamara, the worst
political crook in Washington.

"The Spoilers" in film form, in this sense, appeals
to us even more strongly than the book of Rex Beach.
We view the living scenes in which plot and counter-
plot are launched, and watch the principals as they
play their parts, whether behind doors or in the open.
And we view finally that overpowering scene, where
Glenister—man against man and not with advantage

1. From: *The Moving Picture World*, April 3, 1914, pp. 186–87.

—meets his foe in physical combat, and breaks him with his bare hands. It all seems so real and so just that we whisper, between breaths, "Amen."

Director Colin Campbell is entitled to first mention for his able production of the story and fine judgment in assigning the cast. He has been exceedingly happy in filling the parts of Slap-Jack (Jack McDonald), Judge Stillman (Norvel MacGregor), Broncho Kid (Wheeler Oakman) and Struve (W. H. Ryno), which must have worried him much more than by assigning the principal roles. And I must also compliment him on his selection of the man who serves as keeper of the roadhouse. That fellow, as he appears in character, is a fitting bosom friend of the unscrupulous scoundrel, Struve. Just size them up and see how well they harmonize, in visage and otherwise.

William Farnum appears exceedingly well as Glenister, his first venture in photodramatic art. It is a well studied part; for this headstrong young miner, permeated, as he is, with elemental Americanism and not overburdened with the refining influences of polite society, is a mighty hard character to portray, if one views him from the appealing point. He is force personified; a man who takes what he wants—yet is honest withal.

Tom Santschi is a splendid opposite, in the part of McNamara. Indeed, he loses nothing by comparison, and holds the eye at all times when he is on the screen. Dextry is a fitting partner for Glenister, as Frank Clark reveals him, and commands the admiration of the intelligent for fine characterization. Like Slap-Jack he was born for the part.

Miss Kathlyn Williams, in the fine role of Cherry Malotte, appeals to me more strongly than any other character in the cast. In Cherry, I believe Mr. Beach drew the most appealing, if not the central figure of his story. She is by far the most composite character, actuated both by good and evil, in strong surges that touch one's very soul. She is the one character among all of them whose soul bears her above her surroundings, though there is a palpable taint on her career. Miss Williams brings out finely the weak and strong points of her nature. Miss Bessie Eyton as Helen

Chester, the leading part, contributes much to the success of the strong cast.

Stirring views in the production are the blowing up of the Midas mines, the terrific fight between Glenister and McNamara, the gambling and dance scenes in the music hall, the street duel and the realistic struggle between Helen Chester (Miss Eyton) and Struve in the lonely roadside inn. Another scene that keeps one spellbound shows the Broncho Kid coming stealthily on Glenister to shoot him in the back, at Cherry's home, even still more thrilling than that other scene in the dance hall, where he is about to fire at the same man when prevented by his newly found sister, Helen Chester.

William Farnum, Tom Santschi and Bessie Eyton. The scene in the bank from The Spoilers.

"The Spoilers" has been selected as the opening attraction of the new Strand Theater, New York City, about the middle of April. The nine reels comprise three acts and a prologue. The latter shows scenes which explain incidents that occurred before the Beach story opens, such as the departure of Glenister and Dextry for the States, Glenister's renunciation of Cherry and the Cabal at Washington, by McNamara and his accomplices, to rob the miners at Nome.

EDITOR'S NOTE: *Two years after its initial ap-*

The climax of the fight between Farnum and Santschi from The Spoilers.

pearance, The Spoilers was expanded from 9 to 12 reels and reissued. Reviewers conceded that the expansion took place by padding all major scenes in the picture instead of adding additional incidents, as commonly done at the time. The film's debut marked the high point of both director Colin Campbell and the fortunes of the Selig Polyscope Company; Selig was often quoted as saying that he could have retired on the money brought in by this film alone.

12

Mecca of the Motion Picture[1]

Review of the Beginning and Growth of Kinematographic Production in California—Wonderful Development of a Modern Art that Has Builded Cities and Established Great Public Institutions on the West Coast—Views of Studios and Stories of the Players In and About Los Angeles.

COMPILED BY GEORGE BLAISDELL

It was only a little over seven years ago that Frank Boggs at the head of a small company of Selig players came to Los Angeles and established a studio at the corner of Seventh and South Olive Streets. Mr. Boggs was cut down a few years later by the hand of a Japanese religious fanatic. Had he lived until today he would have seen one hundred directors at work in the territory where he was a pioneer, nine of these for his own company; he would have seen a score of concerns making pictures, employing several thousand men and women; he would have seen the motion picture industry in a position where it is conceded by the Los Angeles Chamber of Commerce to rank first in importance in this city of nearly six hundred thousand inhabitants; and he even would have seen the population of Los Angeles double in the seven years. The judgment of Mr. Boggs and his employer has been vindicated in a remarkable degree.

There is in existence no statistics of official authority bearing on the motion picture industry in Los Angeles. The United States Government census experts are now procuring figures, but these will not be

available until the end of the year. Arthur W. Kinney, industrial commissioner of the local Chamber of Commerce, in a formal statement printed during the spring estimated that 15,000 persons in Los Angeles were supported by the industry, with which assertion it is unlikely any one serious will disagree. Mr. Kinney also said that on a conservative estimate the film industry is worth $15,000,000 a year to Los Angeles. If by this somewhat indefinite statement it is intended to imply that this figure represents the sum annually paid in salaries and wages to officials, producers, actors and employes, there will be serious disagreement. An official of the Chamber of Commerce in conversation with the writer said that the figures quoted perhaps were high and that there was a disposition to modify them—that probably $7,500,000 was nearer the exact amount.

Manufacturers and others in a position to know the labor cost connected with the output of one hundred directors very likely will agree that it will be not over five or six million dollars annually, that even the latter figure is high; and it will not be surprising if when Uncle Sam finishes his official quiz it will be found well below the former. In a rapidly expanding industry and in a fast growing community the use of

1. Excerpt from *Moving Picture World*, July 10, 1915, pp. 215-55.

large figures is the rule. It is the natural outgrowth of the spirit of "boost," and no stranger can remain three months in this community composed of a majority of natives of states other than California without feeling its influence, without noting, for instance, the tendency of the press to enlarge upon the wonderful climate of California and apparently to lose no opportunity to call attention under large headlines to untoward weather conditions in other parts of the country. Candor compels the admission, however, that if in Southern California all the conditions for picture-making were as desirable as are the weather and the photographic light there would not be so many feet of film exposed in other parts of the country.

One hears here on every hand the assertion that 75 to 80 per cent of the pictures produced in the United States are exposed in California. Let us see. We have for a beginning the definite figure of one hundred directors. One company employing more than a half a dozen producers requires that each shall turn in at least an average of a thousand feet of finished negative each week. Another with over a dozen directors concedes an average of a thousand feet a week. A third employing between six and twelve does not release on an average of over six or seven hundred feet for each a week. The nature of the work is such that a larger amount would interfere with the particular quality the company desires to maintain. Many feature companies, using elaborate sets, cannot turn out more than a single reel weekly, if they accomplish that. There was a concern recently which extracted from its directors two thousand feet weekly, but that concern is not now doing business. The latter figure may be attainable where all or nearly all scenes are exteriors, and all other factors favor, but there are few producers who will maintain that it is a safe average. All of which will indicate that 125 reels is hardly an underestimate of the amount of finished negative sent east every week from this vicinity. Two hundred thousand feet is a conservative computation of the weekly output of American film manufacturers—it will probably run considerably higher. Under this basis 60 per cent or 62½ per cent would be a more exact estimate of the relation of the output of this community to that of the whole country—which by all means is no mean figure. Thus it will be seen that among the manufacturers of the United States there is a preponderance of opinion in favor of Southern

California as the ideal location for the making of motion pictures.

Great Selig Enterprise

Enduring Monument Erected by Famous Motion Picture Producer in Los Angeles Known as the Selig Zoo—A Remarkable Collection of Wild Animals Splendidly Housed, to be Formally Opened and Dedicated to the Public on July 19.

BY GEORGE BLAISDELL

William N. Selig will go down in motion picture history as the pioneer manufacturer of the Pacific Coast. That fact will have interest for those everywhere who are concerned in matters kinematographic. Among the descendants of the present residents of Los Angeles, however, it is possible and probable that Mr. Selig's work in the realm of natural history will be regarded as his more enduring monument. In the creation of the great Selig Zoo out on the Mission Road, opposite picturesque Eastlake Park, the Chicago film manufacturer has done something more than gratify a hobby; he has done something more than bring together the largest collection of wild animals in the world; he has done something more than to plan for contributing to the entertainment and instruction of the present generation. He has builded for the future. Mr. Selig does not say so; but his chiefs believe it, and point to the fact that his structures are of solid concrete, that the ornate entrance, on which alone $60,000 was spent, should withstand the wear and tear of the elements for a thousand years.

No brief story can do adequate justice to the collection of seven hundred animals and birds which Colonel Selig—the Governor, his employees call him —has brought from the four corners of the earth. While it may be true that the motion picture trade is interested in the Selig Zoo only in so far as that big establishment may be related to the production of pictures, it is also true that it is interested in the doings of one of its best known men when those doings have a public side—and the Selig Zoo has a public side; it is providing facilities for first-hand study of natural history, one of the most interesting factors in the curriculum, and it is also aiding in the preservation from extinction of many of the rarer beasts and fowl.

The thirty-two-acre park comprising the Selig Zoo has been under its present management for three years. Picturegoers of a few years ago will recall "Captain Kate" and "Lost in the Jungle," those thrilling pictures in which Kathlyn Williams and Thomas Santschi were featured and which served to introduce a new brand of courage to followers of the screen. These subjects were made in Florida, at Jacksonville, and the animals used in them were the property of "Big Otto," a showman. The success of the pictures was so marked that Mr. Selig bought the beasts and had them forwarded to Los Angeles, where they served as the nucleus of the present extensive collection. The initial investment was a quarter of a million dollars. An equal amount has been expended since.

Mr. Selig has been in Los Angeles for many weeks giving his personal attention to the completion of arrangements for the official opening of the park, which will be celebrated on the arrival of the Selig Special from Chicago by way of San Francisco and following the exhibitors' convention in the latter city. All the time the film side has never for a moment been obscured. Every morning has found him in the projection room of the Edendale studio going over the work of his nine directors. In the afternoons he has been at the Zoo, his time divided between Thomas A. Persons, general manager of coast studios, and John G. Robinson, superintendent of the Zoo.

The entrance to the Zoo, opposite Eastlake Park, is a thing of beauty. The design was executed by Romanelli, an Italian sculptor; the figures of the animals on the pedestal between the gates were modeled from beasts within the grounds. Work on the buildings was begun a year ago. An immense amount of preliminary labor was necessary; the soil was swampy, and much drainage was required to prepare the foundations for structures of concrete and steel.

Matching the entrance in striking and imposing appearance is the home of the lions and tigers. It is mission style, the great patio in well kept lawn. The home of the elephants, some distance away, is in the same style of architecture. So, too, is the large amusement pavilion. There are many buildings on the grounds, among them the costume rooms, special storage structures, monkey pavilion, animal cages, bear houses, and the many buildings devoted to the sheltering of birds large and small. The offices, near the business entrance, which is at a distance of several hundred feet north on Selig Boulevard, as the finely asphalted portion of Mission Road passing the property is known, are in rustic style. Here on the border of a great grove of eucalyptus trees are the quarters of the officials and directors and scenario writers. Over on the eastern side of the park are the stages where five directors are working—Tom Santschi, George Nicholls, Lloyd Carlton, Marshall Neilan and Mr. Chaudet. There are runs for jungle scenes, caves for illusions, an exact duplicate of a village in Colon, and the large collection of structures known as Bloom Center, the site where are being photographed the rustic comedies produced by Marshall Neilan.

Bloom Center is a village. One may stand in front of the hotel and look down two streets, or should we say roads? There are the Weekly Bugle print shop and the grocery. The print shop is equipped with the orthodox Gordon press and old style cases filled with type. There are a drug store, with regularly labelled bottles and jars; blacksmith's shop, laundry, livery, barber's shop, brewery, and, to complete the picture, a town hall with its op'ry house and a church. Two primitive lampposts add to the atmosphere.

Near the stages is a large concrete dressing room. In the rear of the stages are the extensive carpenter shops, property rooms and quarters for the scenic artists. In the garage are numbered stalls, each employee—official, director, actor or other—owning a machine having his or her individual storage place. Along the southern side are the corrals for the animals other than those in the category of the wild sort. There are stables for the ponies and the many horses, including Sultan, the "high school" animal famous for his "scholarship." Here, too, are quartered the fourteen camels and three dromedaries and the two giraffes. Prince Chan, orang-outang, resides in an electrically heated house. Five of his species are on the way to join him. Toward the entrance are the aviaries where are quartered all manner of fowl and birds from all countries.

Superintendent Robinson showed the World man over the grounds under his supervision and pointed out some of the more notable inmates of this remarkable animal and bird world. He put his hands through the bars and stroked the sleek sides of the lions and the tigers, a mark of friendly recognition which it is said Mr. Selig shares with him. In the main house are one hundred carnivorous or meat-eating animals.

There are thirty-two lions and lionesses. Of Bengal tigers there are eighteen, the largest collection of similar beasts in the world, and as authority for this statement Superintendent Robinson quotes the younger Hagenback. Among fourteen leopards there is one of the black variety, very rare, and certainly of untamed aspect. There are also two clouded leopards, probably the only pair in the country. There are fourteen panthers, also known as pumas and mountain lions.

Of the herbivora there are seven bears of different species and five Asiatic elephants, including a mother with a nursing baby. The pair of giraffes are now fourteen feet in height, having grown six feet in the last year. They are three years old. There are but nine other giraffes in the country. There are six elk, ten sacred cows of India, including three calves born on the grounds; one zebra, three water or Philippine buffalo, one yak—have we heard somewhere of a Doc Yak?—and four kangaroo. There are ten deer, seven llama, and a pair of Russian wild boars. The hay-eating animals total seventy-seven. In the dog kennels are fourteen German boarhounds, which in their native country are used as police dogs. There are four Eskimo dogs, two St. Bernards, three wolves and an Alaskan husky, a wolf-dog. Of squirrels there are many varieties.

On the collection of representatives of the bird family quartered in the Selig Zoo a book might be written. For instance, of cranes there are a pair each of Kaffir crowned, companion, demoselle, Manchurian and Stanley. There are three golden eagles and one of the bald variety. There are many parrots, cockatoos and macaws. Of pheasants there is probably the largest collection in the United States. There are six Impeyan, imported from the Himalayan Mountains. There are four peacock, six Amherst, seven silver, six golden, eleven English, two white, two copper, five Reeves, two Kerfield and twelve versicolor. There are seventy-eight young pheasants of different species. The young pheasants are raised by Japanese silky hens; several of these are used for this sole purpose. In the duck preserve are fifty mallards, eight mandarin, fourteen teal, eight widgeon, two spoonbills and two muscoveys. There are wild geese from Canada and Australia. Of monkeys there are fifty.

Colonel Selig is reticent as to his future plans for picturemaking, other than as those plans may be revealed in his formal announcements. There is no question, however, that he contemplates big things. There is an evidence of this in the enormous stage he will erect on the zoo grounds, for the making of V-L-S-E features as well as subjects for his regular releases. With five directors working at the Zoo, three at Edendale, and with Tom Mix at Las Vegas, N.M., where it is expected he will go, independent of the facilities at the big Chicago home plant, it is extremely plain that the Selig Polyscope Company is an organization most splendidly equipped for picture-making.

The Selig at Edendale

The Edendale establishment of the Selig Polyscope Company is known as the mission studio. It is situated on Alessandro Street and comprises several acres of ground. The land was bought in the latter part of 1909, or rather one-seventh of the present area was secured at that time; on it was a little green building which is still carefully preserved. In the yard is a space twenty feet square covered with cement. This bit, too, is carefully protected from the ruthless hand of progress, for it represents the first stage of the studio. The property is bounded on the two sides bordering on streets by a high mission wall built of solid concrete and set four and a half feet into the ground. The inner side of the wall is covered with ivy. At the base is a solid hedge of geraniums. The Alessandro street entrance is modeled from the famous bell tower of San Gabriel, with its four bells and two vacant spaces. The entrance on the side street is patterned after that of the mission at Santa Barbara.

James L. McGee is manager of the studio and chief aid to Mr. Persons, general manager of Mr. Selig's coast interests. Mr. McGee is one of the two oldest employes of the Selig Company—and Tom Santschi is the other. Both were members of the company that under Frank Boggs left Chicago in the early part of 1908, and they have been on the Pacific Coast ever since.

The executive offices are just inside the Alessandro Street entrance and at the left of the reception room. Mr. McGee and Mr. Selig when in the city have offices to the right. In the center of the yard is the glass inclosed studio, with a stage 50 by 60. Between it and the administration building there is a large pool for water scenes. On the side street are the offices of the three directors—Colin Campbell, Jack Le Saint and

*Colonel William N. Selig feeding Baby May, one of
the many animals that went to make up the Selig
Jungle Zoo.*

Frank Beal. On the remaining side are the projection room, cutting room, garage and property room, which is 75 by 60. There is a mezzanine floor here filled with objects for use in pictures. The wardrobe adjoins. The carpenters' shop, which also contains the paint frames, is also 75 by 60 in size.

In the rear of the inclosed studio is the back stage, with an area of 60 by 60 feet. Adjoining it is a large property yard, where were seen many evidences of the magnitude of the coming production of "Mizpah." Work on this elaborate subject was to begin about July 1. In several respects it will be the most pretentious picture the Selig Company has undertaken.

Viewed either from the interior of the yard or from without, the Edendale studio of the Selig Company is one of the most picturesque in the country—and if there be any error in that statement it is on the side of conservatism.

There is a third Selig studio in Los Angeles, at Glendale, where Tom Mix, the man who takes long chances, has been directing western subjects. At the time of writing the probabilities were that Mr. Mix would be transferred to a studio at Las Vegas, which location has practically been decided on as the results of a long trip of investigation by General Manager Persons.

Recently a "home-coming" was enjoyed at the newly opened Selig Jungle Zoo, at Los Angeles, and more than six hundred employees, including directors, actors, together with their relatives and friends, were there to accord sincere testimonials of love and respect to the beloved president of the company. The Selig employees of the Mission Studio gave Colonel Selig a magnificent loving cup, suitably engraved as follows: "Hoping the Opening of the Gates Today Will Symbolize Future and Greater Success.—Edendale

Studio." Employees of the Jungle Zoo gave Colonel Selig a massive bronze art work—an elephant attacked by two Bengal tigers.

When one thinks of the Selig activities on the Coast and the great advances made during the last few years, the attractive personality of Kathlyn Williams naturally comes to mind. By winning the regard of the public wherever pictures are shown, and helping to create the demand for Selig subjects, she surely has done her share towards making new and larger studios a profitable investment. A director has yet to propose a wild animal picture in which Miss Williams was afraid to appear, for she is as fearless an actress as ever posed before a camera, and any number of photoplays stand as a testimony to her versatility and her exceptional ability in dramatic roles. Her last, and no doubt, one of her most notable accomplishments, was her strongly emotional characterization of Vera Wilton in Edward E. Rose's "The Rosary."

The Richest Girl in the World. *Guy Oliver, Stella Razetto. January 13, 1915.*

The Spirit of the Violin. *Stella Razetto, Baby Lillian Wade. January 25, 1915.*

The Passer-By. *Stella Razetto. February 8, 1915.*

The Vision of the Shepard. *Kathlyn Williams, Wheeler Oakman. February 1, 1915.*

The Black Diamond. *Guy Oliver. February 17, 1915.*

The Lady of Cyclamen. *Stella Razetto, Guy Oliver,*
George Hernandez. March 8, 1915.

The Poetic Justice of Omar Khan. *Stella Razetto.*
April 12, 1915. 2 reels.

The Carpet of Bagdad. *Wheeler Oakman, Kathlyn Williams, Charles Clary. May 3, 1915. 5 reels.*

The Blood Yoke. *Stella Razetto, Guy Oliver. May 31, 1915. 2 reels.*

His Father's Rifle. *Earle Foxe. June 17, 1915. 3 reels.*

The Fortunes of Marian. *Stella Razetto, Charles Clary.*
June 21, 1915. 2 reels.

The Sands of Time. *Martha Boucher. June 24, 1915.*
3 reels.

The Rosary. *Anna Dodge, Wheeler Oakman, Charles Clary. June 28, 1915. 7 reels.*

Smouldering. *Frank Mayo, Eugenie Besserer. July 12, 1915. 2 reels.*

Ebbtide. *Kathlyn Williams, Wheeler Oakman, Martha Boucher, Harry Lonsdale. July 8, 1915. 3 reels.*

The Unfinished Portrait. *Stella Razetto, Lamar Johnstone. July 26, 1915. 2 reels.*

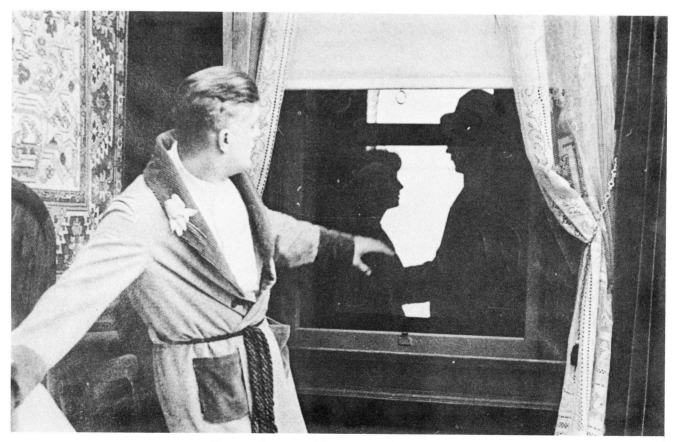

Jimmy. *Lamar Johnstone. July 28, 1915.*

The Melody of Doom. *Eugenie Besserer. August 2, 1915.*

The Face in the Mirror. *Joe King, Stella Razetto, Lamar Johnstone. August 9, 1915. 2 reels.*

The House of a Thousand Candles. *Grace Darmond,*
Harry Mestayer. August 23, 1915. 6 reels.

The Way of a Woman's Heart. *Eugenie Besserer,*
Charles Clary. August 30, 1915. 2 reels.

The Circular Staircase. *Stella Razetto, Jane Watson.*
September 20, 1915. 5 reels.

Mutiny in the Jungle. *Ann Luther. October 2, 1915.*

The Bridge of Time. *Guy Oliver, Virginia Kirtley, Eugenie Besserer. October 7, 1915. 2 reels.*

A Black Sheep. *Grace Darmond, Otis Harlan. October 18, 1915. 5 reels.*

Sweet Alyssum. *Tyrone Power, Kathlyn Williams.*
November 15, 1915. 5 reels.

Thou Shalt Not Covet. *Guy Oliver, Kathlyn Williams.*
February 7, 1916. 5 reels.

The Cycle of Fate. *Bessie Eyton, Lew Cody. April 3, 1916. 5 reels.*

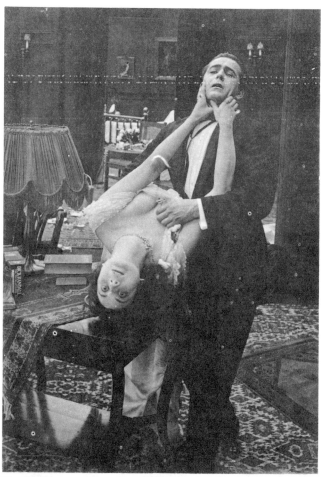

Unto Those Who Sin. *Fritzie Brunette (her debut), George Larkin. March 6, 1916. 5 reels.*

At Piney Ridge. *Vivian Reed, Fritzie Brunette. May 1, 1916. 5 reels.*

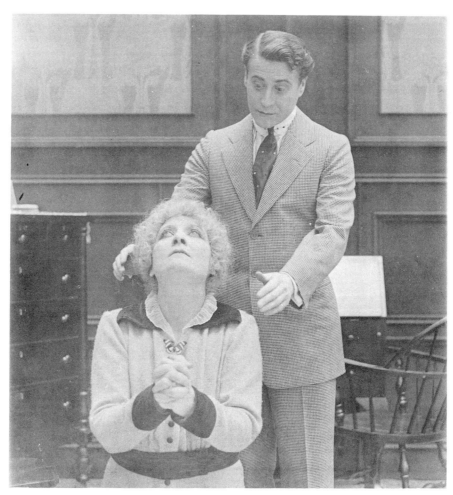

The Sacrifice. *Eugenie Besserer, Harry Mestayer. June 26, 1916. 3 reels.*

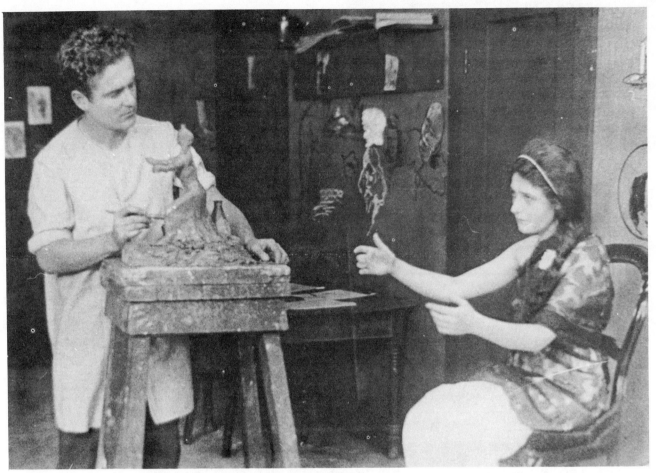

A Prince Chap. *Marshall Neilan, Mary Charleson.*
July 24, 1916. 5 reels.

The Country that God Forgot. *Joseph Girard, Mary*
Charleson. August 21, 1916. 5 reels.

The Crisis. *Tom Santschi, Bessie Eyton. September 1916. Colin Campbell's 10-reel answer to Griffith's* The Birth of a Nation, *adapted from the book by Winston Churchill.*

The Crisis. *Bessie Eyton, Sam Drane as Lincoln, Tom Santschi. September 1916.*

13

William N. Selig Perfects Strong Organization[1]

President of Polyscope Company Feels That He May Take A Rest From the Exacting Requirements of His Large Enterprises Whenever He May Desire With Assurance of Everything Running Smoothly—Berst Accomplishes Gratifying Results with Inauguration of New Policies

William N. Selig, president of the Selig Polyscope Company, one fine day took an inventory of the company which he founded and which he upbuilded to its present state of achievement. Along about that time the preliminary plans for the V-L-S-E, Inc., were being formulated.

"Here," said Colonel Selig to himself, "the burden of administrative affairs are becoming too heavy for me to carry; when the V-L-S-E is started there will be altogether too much business for one individual to transact. We must have new producers and additional actors, in order to carry along our feature program, as well as to keep our regular program up to its present high standard.

"I need a man to look after all these things; I need someone deep in the knowledge of the film business; a man who also knows the technical side of motion picture making; a man in whom I can repose trust and who will carry along the large business enterprises of the Selig Company whenever I should feel that I need a complete rest."

Then it was that Colonel Selig put across another of his sudden surprises. He engaged J. A. Berst as vice-president and general manager. He gave Mr. Berst carte blanch; told him to go ahead, and Mr. Berst has gone ahead.

He has rejuvenated where rejuvenation was deemed necessary because of the important changes in the film manufacturing company, but he has also retained those artists in various lines of the film industry who in the past have proven themselves worthy of the confidence of the Selig company.

Accomplish Big Results

When two such men as Messrs. Selig and Berst co-operate there are certain to be decisive and beneficial results. Working shoulder to shoulder, they have indeed accomplished wonders, and, in the few brief weeks of their collaboration, many and important changes have occurred in the ranks of the Selig company and the new blood injected is making its presence felt in all lines of the film world.

1. From: *Motion Picture News.* Vol. 12. No. 4. July 31, 1915. p. 55.

Others are keeping an eye on the rapid succession of accomplishments being registered by the "Diamond S" outfit not the least of these being the releases which for strength of story, careful production, clear photography, and artistic acting are not surpassed right now in Filmland.

When the administrative shifts were being made the Selig Company started on a still hunt for the best directors and stage stars that money could supply.

Many such have been engaged within the past few weeks and these together with the directors and artists retained by the Selig company are given every convenience in order to enable them to do noteworthy work.

Gratifying results are already beginning to manifest themselves. There is Colin Campbell, dean of the producing corps, whose production of "The Spoilers" set a new standard; Edward J. LeSaint; Thomas Santschi, producer and star; Guy Oliver and Tom Mix, who produces and stars in Selig western dramas and whose dare-devil feats of horsemanship have thrilled the multitudes. These directors are producing worthy productions. The new producers signed by the Selig company within a few weeks are all men of high standing in the ranks of their difficult profession and the list of names is one of which any motion picture company could well be proud.

There is Marshall Neilan, producer and actor; T. N. Heffron, in charge of production at the Chicago studios, who is specializing in Red Seal plays; Louis W. Chaudet; Frank Beal, and George O. Nichols. All are hard at work producing Selig films of quality. And it was not only in the producing end where the stimulus to the hardest kind of artistic work is being felt. Both Messers. Selig and Berst believe that the story, the plot of the picture play is the foundation for the entire structure. In other words, they agree that if the story or plot is weak, then no matter how beautiful the acting or how artistic the direction of the picture play, there will be something sadly lacking.

Other Producers

Lanier Bartlett is another veteran author and editor long exclusively engaged by the Selig Polyscope Company. He wrote "Ebb Tide," that noteworthy Selig Diamond Special in three reels, adapted "The Ne'er-Do-Well" for the screen, and accompanied Colonel Selig and a company of players to the Canal Zone where the scenes in Rex Beach's novel were taken.

Wallace Clifton is Pacific coast editor for the Selig company, has written hundreds of picture play stories, and is particularly happy in the writing of wild animal comedies and dramas. Emma Bell, another versatile editor and author, is employed in the Selig Pacific coast editorial department.

In Chicago Clarence A. Frambers, successful as a writer, is engaged as Eastern Scenario reader, and C. H. Lippert, another versatile writer, is at work at the Selig Chicago studios.

14

Selig Polyscope Studios in Chicago Opened on 6th[1]

Plant After a Shut-Down of Several Months Becomes a Scene of Activity with Production of "The Crisis," Under Colin Campbell

After being closed for several months because of Winter weather, the Selig Polyscope studios in Chicago were opened on Monday, March 6 and there are scenes of great activity at the big Chicago plant.

Colin Campbell, dean of the Selig corps of directors, has been transferred from the Selig Los Angeles studios to the Chicago studios and has commenced active production of the Selig spectacular drama, "The Crisis."

"The Spoilers," "The Ne'er-Do-Well," and other Selig plays will be outdone, according to the plans formulated by Mr. Selig, who is devoting much of his personal attention to the details of production of "The Crisis."

Bessie Eyton, Thomas Santschi, Eugenie Besserer and other Selig stars arrived from Los Angeles the week of February 28 and were joined by several distinguished New York artists. A large stock company was previously held in readiness and active work has started.

Colin Campbell is the director who produced "The Spoilers," "The Ne'er-Do-Well," and "Thou Shalt Not Covet," and it can be said that the best talent

available has been secured to make "The Crisis" the very last word in massive productions.

Three cars loaded with special properties, costumes, armament peculiar to the days of '61, arrived at the Chicago studios last week and a large force of scenic artists have been working for weeks on interior sets.

Thousands of supernumeraries have been engaged to work in spectacular scenes called for in Winston Churchill's novel.

The Chicago newspapers have made much of the fact that this is the first visit ever paid by Miss Eyton, a motion picture star of international renown, to Chicago.

Miss Eyton, previous to this visit to Chicago, never placed her dainty foot outside the confines of California. She was given a cordial reception by her Chicago friends and admirers.

It was seven long years ago that Thomas Santschi left Chicago with a pioneer company of Selig players for the Pacific Coast.

Since that time, he has never returned to Chicago, the scene of his initial motion picture triumphs, until he arrived to enact the leading role of Stephen Brice in "The Crisis."

Eugenie Besserer owns a pretty home in Los Angeles and was loath to leave that home, but she cheerfully

---

1. From: *The Motion Picture News*, Vol. 13. No. 11. March 18, 1916, p. 1568.

answered to the call of duty and will enact an important role in the forthcoming Selig drama.

Miss Eyton, while in the spoken drama, supported Wilton Lackeye, McKee Rankin, Margaret Anglin, Frank Keenan and others, and once held the title of the champion lady fencer of the world.

These and other stars have been overwhelmed with invitations to receptions and card parties, for their Chicago friends seem determined to make their sojourn in Chicago a most happy one.

Mr. Selig expects to escort his players to St. Louis, Vicksburg, Miss., and other locations to film scenes called for in "The Crisis."

In St. Louis the court house, the arsenal and the old slave pen will be filmed and the old battle grounds at Vicksburg will also be utilized.

15

Epilogue

The reorganization of staff and facilities referred to in the preceding two articles marked the Selig Polyscope Company's reaction to the beginning of the end. The year 1914 found the feature motion picture gaining in popularity among both exhibitors and patrons, yet most of the pioneer production firms were committed by traditions and financial structure to the shorter films. The combination of Vitagraph, Selig, Lubin and Essanay known as V-L-S-E was an attempt to produce and distribute longer pictures which General Film would not handle. As General Film was not in a healthy condition anyway, V-L-S-E was looked upon as a means of bypassing the trust (which would soon die of its own inertia) and seeking to cure a declining market with the remedy of longer pictures.

V-L-S-E survived for little more than a year, but it never seemed to fully realize its potential. Part of the problem rested in the constant bickering that took place between its chief administrative officers and founders, who never seemed able to agree on exactly what policy the firm should follow. Another part of the problem could be found in the rather boring feature pictures released by its member companies; no outstanding Lubin or Essanay feature picture came from this period. When Vitagraph recapitalized, it dropped out and was replaced by George Kleine, whose similar alliance with Edison had not worked out very well either. K-L-S-E continued through 1917 and then disappeared as first Essanay, then Selig and finally Lubin closed their doors forever and moved into the pages of motion picture history.

The closing down of the Chicago plant during the winter of 1915 was followed soon after by that of the Edendale studio, which was leased on December 1 to William Fox. Remaining Selig production on the West Coast was transferred to the Jungle Zoo and then to Chicago. Although the trade papers for this period are most enthusiastic in their optimistic treatment of the pioneer production companies' future, there were several factors at work which combined to deal the death blow. Shortsighted management contributed to the demise of Essanay and Kalem, whose insistence upon short films remained adamant. The outbreak of war in Europe in 1914 was a large factor; much profit had come from distributing American films abroad. War meant that the market on the continent of Europe was gone and the 1915 War Tax instituted by England meant that each 1000-foot reel of film exported from this country cost its producer $160 to bring into England. While companies like Keystone produced a product sufficiently popular to offset this added expense, the feature dramas of V-L-S-E (and their shorter films) did not merit the trouble or expense involved.

None of the pioneer companies seemed able to compete with the independents, who had finally broken the Motion Picture Patents Company and forged ahead in terms of stories, casts and salesmanship. It almost seemed as if Colonel Selig and his compatriots were tired of the competition and more than willing to drop out. Big pictures like *The Crisis,* which ate up large sums of money, went unnoticed in the face of *The Birth of a Nation, Civilization,* and *Intolerance,* and stars like Kathlyn Williams finally left the fold to join Famous Players, Fox and Universal where their paychecks were elevated by many times what Selig could and would pay.

Finally, Selig himself was a man past 50 who had already made his financial mark and the increasing effort required to keep the Polyscope Company competitive seemed not worth the reward. When Selig finally closed the doors for the last time in 1918, he took his large story file and moved into the field of independent production. The story file had proven a large asset; many times in previous years, he had remade films that had been released earlier at no additional cost to himself for rights and he continued to do so into 1923. Few of the Selig Polyscope films remain in existence today, making it quite difficult to judge exactly what place in cinema history should be assigned to this particular company. However, it is worthy of mention that from Selig came the first true motion picture serial, *The Adventures of Kathlyn,* the immensely popular *The Spoilers* and *The Ne'er-Do-Well,* and the western comedies and dramas of Tom Mix, which provided a lengthy and well-founded apprenticeship for this man soon to become "America's Champion Cowboy" and a legend in his own right.

On the basis of these accomplishments alone, it seems fair to place the Selig Polyscope Company ahead of Kalem, Lubin, Essanay and Edison in importance to the growth of the early motion picture. But the question is an open-ended one that may never be satisfactorily resolved by cinema historians.